FULL CIRCLE

Senior Authors
Carl B. Smith
Virginia A. Arnold

Linguistics Consultant
Ronald Wardhaugh

Macmillan Publishing Co., Inc.
New York

Collier Macmillan Publishers
London

ACKNOWLEDGMENTS

The publisher gratefully acknowledges permission to reprint the following copyrighted material:

"Adventures of Isabel," from *The Face is Familiar* by Ogden Nash. Copyright © 1936 by Ogden Nash. Published in England in *Parents Keep Out* by Ogden Nash. Reprinted by permission of Little, Browen and Co. and the Estate of Ogden Nash.

"Butterfly Wings," from *In the Woods, In the Meadow, In the Sky* by Aileen Fisher. Copyright © 1965 by Aileen Fisher. Reprinted by permission of Charles Scribner's Sons.

"The Case of the Whistling Ghost," from *Encyclopedia Brown Gets His Man* by Donald J. Sobol. Copyright © 1967 by Donald J. Sobol. Reprinted by permission of the Publisher, E. P. Dutton, Inc.

"Don't tell me that I talk too much," from *And the Frog Went Blah* by Arnold Spilka. Copyright © 1972 by Arnold Spilka. Reprinted by permission of Charles Scribner's Sons.

"The Girl Who Found a Dragon," from *Dinosaurs* by Darlene Geis. Copyright © 1969 by Grosset & Dunlap, Inc. Published by Grosset & Dunlap, Inc.

"The Great Fish," adapted from *The Great Fish* by Peter Parnall. Copyright © 1973 by Peter Parnall. Reprinted by permission of Doubleday & Company, Inc.

"Growing Time," adapted from *Growing Time* by Sandol Stoddard Warburg. Copyright © 1969 by Sandol S. Dollard. Copyright © 1969 by Leonard Weisgard. Reprinted by permission of Houghton Mifflin Company.

"Harlequin and the Gift of Many Colors," adapted from *Harlequin and the Gift of Many Colors* by Remy Charlip and Burton Supree. Copyright © 1973 by Remy Charlip and Burton Supree. All rights reserved. Published by Parents' Magazine Press. Reprinted by permission of Arthur D. Zinberg, Esq., 11 East 44th Street, New York, New York 10017.

"A hippo yawned," from *A Rumbudgin of Nonsense* by Arnold Spilka. Copyright © 1970 by Arnold Spilka. Reprinted by permission of Charles Scribner's Sons.

"I know a man . . . ," "Watch Out . . . ," and "I bet I can . . . ," from *Tomfoolery: Trickery and Foolery with Words* by Alvin Schwartz. Reprinted by permission of J.B. Lippincott Company and Curtis Brown, Ltd. "There were two skunks . . ." and "Ask me if I'm a boat," from Louis C. Jones Archives and Harold W. Thompson Archives, New York State Historical Association, New York. "What does a duck do . . . ?" reprinted by permission of Ms. Barbara Crampton and the Maryland Folklore Archives, University of Maryland. "Pete and Repeat . . . ," from Library of Congress Archives, WPA Folklore Archives. "I keep seeing spots before my eyes . . . ," "Knock, Knock . . . red who," "Knock, knock . . . hatch who . . . ," from *Over 1000 Jokes by Cracky*. Copyright © 1969 by Western Publishing Company, Inc. Reprinted by permission. "Do you know what Tommy . . . ," "Sammy? . . . ," "Say, Daddy owl . . . ," and "What does a two-hundred-pound . . . ," from *Jokes, Puns and Riddles* by David Allen Clark. Copyright © 1968 by Doubleday & Company. Reprinted by permission.

This work is also published in individual volumes under the titles: *Beginnings* and *Endings,* copyright © 1983 Macmillan Publishing Co., Inc. Parts of this work were published in earlier editions of SERIES r.

Macmillan Publishing Co., Inc.
866 Third Avenue, New York, New York 10022
Collier Macmillan Canada, Inc.

Printed in the United States of America
ISBN 0-02-131800-X
9 8 7 6 5 4

Contents

5

BEGINNINGS

When you have finished one thing, it's time to start something new. Sometimes something you do may not work right. Then it's time to start over. There are always new ways to do things. If you think about the things you do, you may find new ways to do these things.

In "Beginnings," you will read about a girl and her grandfather who try something new. You will read about two girls who speak different languages and find a way to talk to each other. As you read, see if you can think of other ways to do the things you read about. Would your way work as well?

Phoebe's First Duet

Judith Davis

I never missed a party at Grandpa Theo's. All my aunts, uncles, and cousins were there. All Grandpa Theo's friends and music pupils came, too.

The table was covered with good food. People talked and laughed and sang. Sometimes Uncle Dimitri pulled out his handkerchief. He took Aunt Myra's hand, and Grandpa Theo took Grandma's hand. Then they did the snake dance. We all joined hands and lined up behind them. We wound in and out, dancing the slow snake dance.

Then Grandpa Theo opened the piano. Everyone was quiet. "Phoebe," he called to me, "please turn the pages for us."

Grandpa Theo sat down with one of his pupils. They played wonderful music together, while I turned the pages. I was learning to play the piano with Grandpa Theo, so that someday I would be ready to play a duet with him.

But then things changed. I knew something was wrong when Grandpa didn't have music parties very often. Grandpa Theo didn't sing and he didn't dance. His pupils played duets without him. When the parties stopped for good, I knew something was really wrong. Later, even my piano lessons stopped.

Grandpa Theo didn't like to talk about it. But I knew he had trouble hearing. If he didn't watch me when I talked, he sometimes wouldn't even answer me. Other times he wouldn't laugh when I said something funny.

He turned the radio on too loudly. People had to shout when they wanted to talk to him. I had to pat his shoulder to get him to look at me when I talked. But he just didn't talk with me very much any more.

Whenever we visited Grandpa Theo, my mother would say, "Papa, why don't you go get a hearing test? Maybe you need a hearing aid."

But Grandpa wouldn't go. He wouldn't listen to her. One day, when we were visiting, my mother told him again to get a hearing test.

Grandpa Theo said, "I have always taken care of myself. I'll go on taking care of myself, too. Anyway, why should I look foolish?"

"You wouldn't look foolish, Papa," my mother said. "It's not foolish to hear better." But Grandpa didn't hear her. He went out to the garden to be alone.

I felt very sad. "I wish Grandpa Theo could hear better," I told my mother. "I really miss all the things we used to do together."

"Why don't you go out and tell him that, Phoebe?" my mother asked.

So I went out to the garden. I found
Grandpa Theo sitting under the fig tree,
looking up at the pretty leaves. I patted
his shoulder. He looked at me.

"Grandpa Theo, I really miss our talks and your songs and your parties. I miss my piano lessons, too. Maybe a hearing aid would help you hear better, and we could do those things again. Why won't you even try?"

Grandpa Theo stared at me. It was so quiet in the garden that I could hear a leaf fall from the tree.

"Maybe you're right, Phoebe," he said slowly. "I could try. I guess I was thinking only of myself." Then he smiled at me and took my hand. "Are you still playing the piano?" he asked.

"Yes, Grandpa Theo, but it's not the same."

"Do you remember to play one hand at a time, and then both hands together?"

"Yes, Grandpa Theo."

"Do you play each piece slowly at first?" he asked.

"Sometimes," I said, "but I like to play fast."

"Yes, you play well," Grandpa Theo said. "You should be ready for a duet soon."

Something inside me jumped. For a minute I couldn't say a thing. I just looked at Grandpa Theo.

"Phoebe," said Grandpa Theo, "I miss your lessons, too. I just wasn't thinking about the important things. But now I'm going to get a hearing test, and I'd like you to come with me."

"Oh, Grandpa Theo!" I shouted, and I gave him a big hug. I felt like singing.

"If a hearing aid can help," he said, "you shall play your first duet soon."

Three days later, we went to see Dr. Grant. She asked Grandpa a lot of questions. Then she gave Grandpa some earphones.

"These earphones will test your hearing," she said. "I'll test one ear at a time. As soon as you can hear a sound in the earphones, press this button." She showed Grandpa Theo where the button was.

"Then I'll make the sound louder, so you can hear it very well," Dr. Grant said. "After that, I'll make it softer and softer, until you can't hear it any more. I'll do this many times, until I know just when you start to hear the sound. Are you ready?"

Grandpa Theo nodded and put the earphones on. I smiled at him.

Dr. Grant gave Grandpa Theo a lot of different tests. When they were all done, she sat down to talk with us again.

"You are lucky," she said. "A hearing aid makes sounds louder. Right now, that's all you need to hear better."

Grandpa Theo gave a big sigh and smiled. Then Dr. Grant showed him all the different kinds of hearing aids. One of them looked like a little radio. It had wires coming out of it, with little earplugs at the ends of the wires.

Another one could be put onto eyeglasses, and another one went on the back of the ear.

Dr. Grant gave Grandpa the kind that looked like a radio. "Try this one."

"This doesn't look so bad," said Grandpa Theo. "Phoebe, go to the other side of the room and say something, and I will try my new hearing aid."

"When can we start playing?" I asked from the other side of the room.

"Today!" cried Grandpa Theo. "I can hear you very well! We've got a lot of work to do. You must get ready for your first duet."

19

"May I listen through your hearing aid?" I asked.

Grandpa Theo looked at Dr. Grant. She nodded, so Grandpa gave me the hearing aid. I listened through it. It really made everything sound loud. Then I gave it back to Grandpa Theo.

"You must go slowly at first," said Dr. Grant, smiling. "Wear the hearing aid a little longer each day, until you are used to it. Take good care of it, and it will work well for you, like any other tool. Good luck with your duet. Let me know how you do."

"Thank you, Dr. Grant," said Grandpa Theo. We shook hands all around.

Grandpa Theo used the hearing aid a little longer each day. "It helps me when I'm playing the piano," he said. "But it picks up all kinds of sounds. Sudden sounds or loud ones are hard to take.

When there are too many loud sounds at once, I just turn it off."

In time, Grandpa Theo got used to his hearing aid. He began to like it very much.

During that time, I learned my first duet. We played the duet for everyone at Grandpa Theo's next music party. This time, one of my cousins turned the pages!

WHAT'S THE MATTER WITH THURMAN?

Dina Anastasio

Thurman's life was very good. The pond in which he lived was clean and cool. The countryside was peaceful and quiet. And, best of all, Thurman had more friends than he knew what to do with.

Oh, he had problems, of course, for he was very small, like all tadpoles. Snakes, fish, and even frogs, were always trying to catch him for dinner. But they never caught Thurman. He was much too fast and clever for them.

Thurman was the biggest and the smartest of all the tadpoles in the pond. And he soon became the leader.

Day after day, hour after hour, Thurman swam up and down the pond in search of something to eat.

22

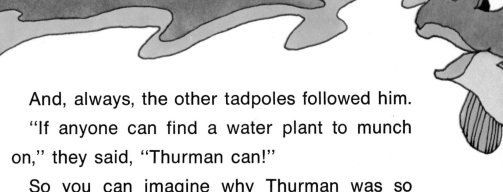

And, always, the other tadpoles followed him.

"If anyone can find a water plant to munch on," they said, "Thurman can!"

So you can imagine why Thurman was so well thought of in his peaceful pond.

Up and down they swam, hiding from enemies and searching for food. As they swam, they drank mouthfuls of water. The water passed back through the gills inside their heads. In this way they breathed, taking air from the water with their gills. Then they blew the water out of holes on the side of their heads—just like a fish.

When Thurman was about two months old, a strange thing happened. He was swimming along one peaceful day in search of food. All of a sudden the sound of laughter echoed behind him. Of course, tadpoles don't really laugh, so you'll have to imagine a little bit here. It was clear to Thurman that *something* was strange.

Shaking his tail, Thurman flipped around and faced his friends.

"What's so funny?" Thurman asked, smiling, for he was always ready for a good laugh.

But no one answered. They just sat there, staring at Thurman. Then they all swam away.

Poor Thurman! He had no idea what was wrong. But that something was indeed wrong was *very* clear.

Thurman was miserable! All day long he swam around alone. He thought about the other tadpoles who had once been his friends.

Toward dark, a tiny little tadpole swam up to Thurman.

"Hi, Thurman!" he said.

"I thought no one was speaking to me," said Thurman sadly.

The little tadpole had not heard of Thurman's troubles, and so he stayed to play. But it was not long before he too noticed something odd about Thurman. Then he began to laugh.

"What *is* it?" cried Thurman.

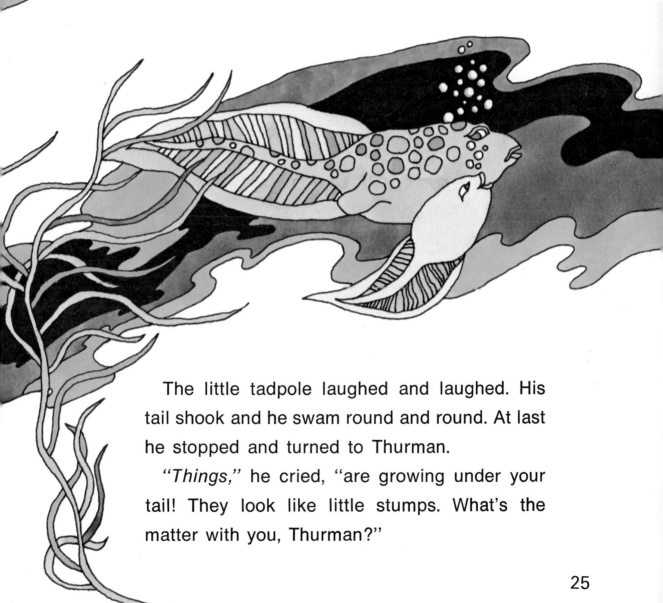

The little tadpole laughed and laughed. His tail shook and he swam round and round. At last he stopped and turned to Thurman.

"*Things,*" he cried, "are growing under your tail! They look like little stumps. What's the matter with you, Thurman?"

And then, without waiting for an answer, the little tadpole swam away.

Poor Thurman! He didn't know what was happening to him. He flicked his tail and—yes —something was indeed growing under his tail.

Although Thurman didn't know it, something wonderful was happening to him.

Thurman Tadpole was becoming a frog! And those two little stumps were the beginnings of what would soon become two nice long legs.

But of course *Thurman* didn't know any of this. All Thurman knew was that he was now different from the other tadpoles. He was very lonely.

And so poor Thurman played alone for what seemed like forever, but was really only about a month.

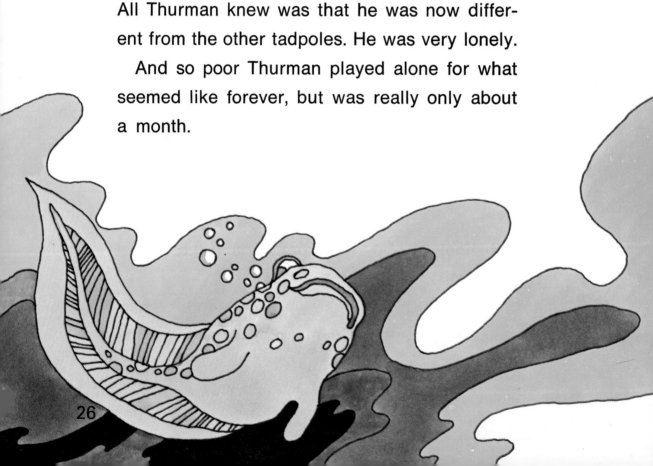

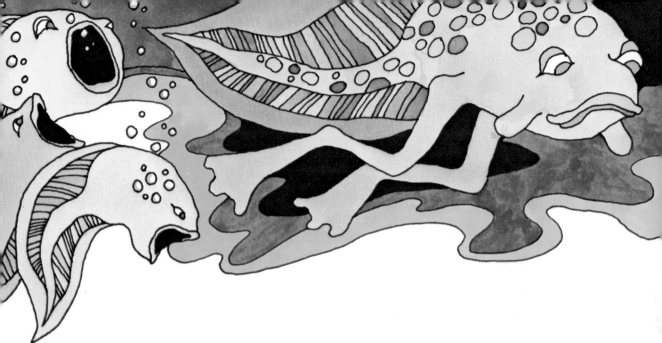

And throughout it all, Thurman changed. As his back legs grew, his front legs began to form behind the gills under his skin. One day one of these front legs popped out of his gill hole. This really made the other tadpoles laugh.

"What's the matter with Thurman?" they asked as he began to look stranger and stranger.

The more he changed, the more unhappy poor Thurman became. The other tadpoles either laughed at him or didn't speak to him at all.

And Thurman's life was miserable.

Thurman was *very* unhappy.

Soon Thurman's other leg popped out. He began to look more and more like a frog. But Thurman wasn't only changing on the outside.

He was also becoming a frog on the inside.

His gills changed to lungs, which meant that Thurman had to swim up to breathe air. His mouth became bony, so that he would be able to eat bugs instead of water plants. While this was happening, Thurman didn't eat at all. He lived on food which was stored in his tail. As Thurman's teeth formed, his tail shrank until, at last, it was a stump. Thurman had become a frog!

Of course, by this time, all of the other tadpoles had changed, too. But not one had changed as much as Thurman. So they still laughed and asked, "What's the matter with Thurman?" And Thurman was very sad!

One day, when Thurman's tail had disappeared and his skin had turned dark green, he decided to try out his new legs. With one big jump, he hopped out of the water and onto a nearby rock. With his big eyes he took in the world around him. Then he looked down into the water at the tadpoles who used to be his friends. And, for the first time in his life, Thurman felt sorry for someone other than himself. They too would soon discover this wonderful world outside their pond. But right now they were still, in many ways, just fish. But he—Thurman Tadpole—was a fine, fat frog!

Thurman laughed and waved, and with one very high jump, he hopped off to explore his new world.

YOU, YOU, CARIBOU

The caribou is a kind of deer that the Eskimos have depended on for many years. This poem about a caribou is by an Eskimo hunter. It was spoken to a Danish man who wrote it down in his own language. Later, the poem was changed into English, the language we speak.

You, you, caribou
yes you
long legs
yes you
long ears
you with the long neck hair—
From far off you're little as a louse;
Be my swan, fly to me, long horns
waving great bull
cari-bou-bou-bou.

Put your footprints on this land,
this land I'm standing on,
So rich with the lichens you love.
See, I'm holding in my hand
the reindeer moss you're dreaming of—
So delicious yum, yum, yum—
Come, caribou, come.

Come on, move those bones,
move your leg bones back and forth
and give yourself to me.
I'm here,
I'm waiting just for you
you, you, caribou.
APPEAR.
COME HERE.

—An Eskimo Poem

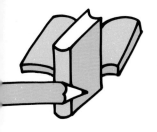

How Did the Writer Feel?

As you read a story carefully, you may be able to understand more than just the words. You may be able to tell how the writer felt when writing the story. Read the sentences below. Think how the writer may have felt about Betsy while writing the story.

Story 1 Betsy is a wonderful girl. She is lots of fun. She smiles at people. Everyone likes her. She is also the best baseball player in our school.

How did the writer feel about Betsy? Write the answer on your paper.

> **a.** The writer never knew Betsy.
> **b.** The writer did not like Betsy.
> c. The writer really liked Betsy.

Now read each story on the next page. Think how the writer may have felt while writing the story. Choose an answer that tells how the writer may have felt. Write the answer on your paper.

Story 2   I could look all day at birds flying in the sky. Birds have such beautiful feathers. They make such lovely sounds when they sing and talk to one another. Sometimes I try to sing and talk with birds.

   a. The writer did not really like birds.

   b. The writer knew nothing about birds.

   c. The writer really liked birds.

Story 3   Slugs are ugly creatures. When you touch them, they feel like awful worms. Slugs eat the vegetables in people's gardens. But what would want to eat a slug?

   a. The writer really liked slugs.

   b. The writer wanted slugs for pets.

   c. The writer was disgusted with slugs.

Story 4   Andy always wants to have his own way. He always wants to be first in line. He always wants to win. Now he's broken my new game!

   a. The writer did not know Andy.

   b. The writer was disgusted with Andy.

   c. The writer never thought about Andy.

The Rooster Who Understood Japanese

Yoshiko Uchida

Part One

Mr. Lincoln's Crowing

"Mrs. K.!" Miyo called. "I'm here!" Every afternoon when Miyo came home from school, she went to the home of her neighbor, Mrs. Kitamura. Miyo called her "Mrs. K."

Miyo's mother was a doctor and didn't get home until supper time. Sometimes she didn't get home even then. If she didn't, Miyo just stayed on at Mrs. K's.

Mrs. Kitamura was a widow, and she enjoyed Miyo's company. Not that she was lonely. She had a dog named Jefferson, a ten-year-old parrot named Hamilton, a black cat named Leonardo, and a pet rooster named Mr. Lincoln. She talked to all of them in Japanese. She also talked to the onions and potatoes she'd planted in her front yard. She asked them each day to grow plump and delicious.

About the time Miyo came home from school, Mrs. K. was usually outside talking to her potatoes and onions. But today Mrs. K. was nowhere to be seen. She wasn't out front, and she wasn't in back talking to any of her animals either.

Her dog, Jefferson, came to greet Miyo as she opened the gate.

"Hello, Jefferson Kitamura," Miyo said. "Where's Mrs. K.?"

Jefferson wagged his tail and sniffed at Miyo. Then he went back to his special spot at the foot of the willow tree.

Miyo stopped next to see Mr. Lincoln. He was strutting about in his pen. He was making rooster-like sounds and looking very intelligent. Mrs. K. had told Miyo that Mr. Lincoln understood every word she said to him whether she spoke in English or Japanese.

"Mrs. Kitamura, *doko*?" Miyo said, asking Mr. Lincoln where she was.

He cocked his head and looked at her with his small bright eyes. Then he made a squawking sound.

"Maybe Mr. Lincoln does understand Japanese," Miyo thought. "But it certainly doesn't do me any good if I can't understand what he says back to me."

"Never mind," she said aloud. "I'll find her." She hurried toward the house. The back door was open, and Miyo walked in.

"Mrs. K., I'm here!" she called once more.

A high voice repeated, "Mrs. K., I'm here." It was Hamilton, the parrot. He lived in a big gold cage in Mrs. Kitamura's kitchen.

"Hello, Hamilton," Miyo said.

"Hello, Hamilton," he answered back.

Miyo sniffed as she walked through the kitchen. She was hoping she might smell brownies or freshly baked bread. But today there was only the smell of floor wax.

Miyo went through the swinging doors into the dining room. She found Mrs. K. sitting at the big dining–room table. She was doing something Miyo had never seen her do before. She was making herself a cup of ceremonial tea.

Miyo knew what Mrs. K. was doing. She had seen a lady in a pretty kimono perform the Japanese tea ceremony just last month.

Somehow Mrs. K. didn't look quite right. She was preparing the tea in her gardening clothes. She was sitting at a table piled high with old newspapers. She was frowning, too.

Miyo knew the tea ceremony helped to make one feel peaceful and calm.

"Mah!" Mrs. K. said, looking surprised. "I was so busy with my thoughts that I didn't even hear you come in."

Miyo looked at the light, green tea in the tea bowl. She knew it was strong and bitter. "Is that our afternoon tea?" she asked, trying not to look disappointed.

"No, no, not yours," Mrs. K. answered quickly. "Just mine. I make it to calm myself." Then she turned the bowl around carefully and drank it. She drank it in the proper three and a half sips. "There," she sighed.

"Are you calm now?" Miyo asked.

Mrs. K. shook her head. "Not really. As a matter of fact, I am most upset."

Mrs. Kitamura stood up and started toward the kitchen. Usually she was full of fun, but today she hardly smiled at Miyo.

"I've been upset since seven o'clock this morning," she explained suddenly.

"Why?" Miyo asked.

"It's my new neighbor, Mr. Wickett," Mrs. K. said. "He told me that if Mr. Lincoln didn't stop waking him up by crowing at six in the morning, he was going to report me to the police for disturbing the peace! Can you imagine anything so unfriendly?"

Miyo certainly couldn't. "He's mean," she said.

"What am I going to do?" Mrs. K. sighed. "I can't tell Mr. Lincoln he is not to crow anymore. That would be like telling Jefferson not to wag his tail, or telling Leonardo not to groom himself..."

"Or telling Hamilton not to copy us," Miyo said.

"You're right," Mrs. K. agreed. "He is only acting in his natural rooster-like way.

Anyway, everyone should be up by six o'clock."

Miyo wondered what she could say to make Mrs. K. feel better. "I'll ask my mother. She'll know what to do," Miyo said as she left Mrs. Kitamura's house.

Mrs. K. nodded. "I hope so," she said sadly. "In the meantime, I must think of something before six o'clock tomorrow morning."

When Miyo got home, Mother was just starting supper. "Hi, sweetie," she called. "How was Mrs. K.?"

"She was worried," Miyo answered as she began to set the table. "She's got to make Mr. Lincoln stop crowing."

"Whatever for?"

Miyo quickly told Mother about Mr. Wickett. "He's mean," she said, frowning at the thought of him. "Mr. Lincoln doesn't hurt anybody."

But Mother said, "Well, I can see Mr. Wickett's side, too. If I could sleep late, I'm not so sure I'd like having a rooster wake me at six o'clock. Besides," she added, "our town is growing. We're in the city limits now. Maybe Mrs. K. will just have to give Mr. Lincoln away."

Miyo didn't even want to think of such a thing. "But he's not just any old rooster," she said. "Besides," she added, "he doesn't crow very loud."

Mother nodded. "I know," she said. "Well, maybe we can think of something."

But nobody could—not Mother, not Miyo, nor Mrs. K.

Part Two
A Box for Mr. Lincoln

That night Mrs. K. brought Mr. Lincoln inside the house. She put him into a big box in her bedroom.

"Poor Mr. Lincoln," she said to Miyo the next day. "It was hard for him to breathe, and I hardly got any sleep at all. He crowed in the morning anyway. But I don't think Mr. Wickett heard him because so far the police haven't come. But I jump every time my doorbell rings. What on earth are we going to do?"

Miyo wished she had an answer. But all she could say was, "Mama and I are both thinking hard."

Mrs. K. had been so worried she had spent the whole day cooking Japanese food. She thought cooking would take her mind off Mr. Lincoln.

"I made two kinds of osushi today," she said to Miyo. She showed Miyo a huge dish of flavored rice rolled in sheets of seaweed. She had also cooked slices of fried beancurd and filled them with rice.

Mrs. K. gave Miyo a dish of *osushi* when she left. "Take some home for supper," she said. "Your mama will be glad not to have to cook tonight."

Miyo felt that neither she nor her mother really deserved the *osushi*. They hadn't come up with one good idea to help Mrs. K.

"I do wish we could think of a way to help Mrs. K.," Mother said as they ate Mrs. K.'s delicious *osushi*.

But Mother was very tired at the end of a long day looking after sick babies and sick children. She just couldn't find any good ideas inside her head. She did say, however, that keeping Mr. Lincoln inside a box in the house was not the answer.

Mrs. K. certainly found out it wasn't. The next night she brought him inside, and Mr. Lincoln poked his way right out of the box. He walked all over her house. He scratched the floors and pecked at her sofa. He got into a fight with Leonardo, the cat. By the time Mrs. K. got to them, there were feathers all over her living room.

"I suppose I will have to give Mr. Lincoln away," Mrs. K. said sadly. "But I can't give him to just anybody. It has to be someone who will love him." Trying to look brave, she said, "If I can't find a new home for Mr. Lincoln, I suppose I will just have to go to jail."

Miyo thought and thought. How in the world could they find just the right person to take Mr. Lincoln? Then, suddenly, she had an idea.

"I know," she said brightly. "I'll put an ad in our class magazine."

Mrs. K. thought about it. "Well," she said slowly, "I suppose it won't do any harm."

What she really meant was that it probably wouldn't do any good either. But Miyo was determined to try. She made her ad very special. She wrote, "WANTED: NICE HOME FOR FRIENDLY, INTELLIGENT ROOSTER. P.S. HE UNDERSTANDS JAPANESE." Then she added, "PLEASE HURRY!"

Her teacher told her it was a fine ad. He suggested that Miyo put in her phone number, too. Miyo also drew a picture of Mr. Lincoln below her ad. She tried to make him look friendly and intelligent.

The magazine came out on Monday. That very afternoon, a police officer rang the doorbell of Mrs. K.'s house.

"I've a complaint, ma'am," he said, "about a rooster?" He seemed to think there might have been some mistake.

Mrs. K. sighed. "Come inside, officer," she said. "I've been expecting you." She supposed now she would just have to go quietly to jail. But first she wanted a cup of tea. "Would you like some tea?" she asked.

Officer McArdle was tired and his feet hurt. "Thank you, ma'am," he said, and he came inside. He looked all around at Mrs. Kitamura's home. It was full of Japanese things he'd never seen. There were Japanese dolls dancing inside glass cases. There were Japanese paintings hanging on the walls. There were Japanese books and newspapers spread out all over the dining room table.

Mrs. K. brought in some tea and cookies. "Now," she said, "please have some tea, officer." She took off her apron and smoothed down her hair. Then she told Officer McArdle all about her troubles with Mr. Lincoln.

He looked understanding, but he said, "You're breaking a city law by having a rooster in your yard. You really should be fined, you know."

"Even if I am only barely inside the city limits?" Mrs. K. asked.

Officer McArdle nodded. "I'm afraid so. I'll give you two more days to get rid of your rooster. Mr. Wickett says you're disturbing the peace."

Then he thanked her for the tea and cookies, and he was gone.

Part Three
Mr. Lincoln's New Home

Miyo was proud of the ad in her class magazine. But no one seemed at all interested in Mr. Lincoln. Instead, a few people told her how much they liked her feature story. It was about Mr. Botts, the school custodian, who was retiring.

She had written, "Say good-by to the best custodian our school ever had. Mr. Botts is retiring. He and Mrs. Botts are going to Far Creek. He is going to eat a lot and sleep a lot and maybe go fishing. So, so long, Mr. Botts. And good luck!"

Her teacher told her it was a fine story.

On her way home, Miyo ran into Mr. Botts himself. He told her it was the first time in his whole life that anyone had written a feature story about him.

When Mr. Botts got home that night, he took off his shoes and sat in his favorite chair. Then he read the magazine from cover to cover. At the bottom of page twenty, he saw Miyo's ad about Mr. Lincoln.

"Tami," he said to Mrs. Botts, who

happened to be Japanese, "how would you like to have a rooster?"

"A what?"

"A rooster," Mr. Botts repeated. "One that understands Japanese."

Mrs. Botts looked at Mr. Botts with wonder in her eyes. Mr. Botts kept right on talking. "When we move to Far Creek," he said, "didn't you say you were going to grow vegetables and raise chickens while I go hunting and fishing?"

Mrs. Botts remembered having said something like that. "Yes, I guess I did."

"Well, if you're going to raise chickens, you'll need a rooster."

"Why, I guess that's so."

"Then we might as well have one that's intelligent and friendly," Mr. Botts said. Then he went right to the telephone to call Miyo.

"I'll take that rooster you want to find a home for," he said. "My wife, Tami, could talk to it in Japanese, too."

Miyo couldn't believe it. Someone had actually read her ad and that someone was Mr. Botts. They would give Mr. Lincoln a fine home. At last, she had done something to help Mrs. K. As soon as she told Mother, she ran right to tell Mrs. K. the good news.

Mrs. K. was just about to stuff Mr. Lincoln into a wooden box for the night. Miyo told her that Mr. Lincoln would have a nice home in Far Creek with Mr. and Mrs. Botts. Mrs. K. gave Miyo such a hug she almost squeezed the breath out of her.

"Hooray! *Banzai!*" Mrs. K. said happily. "Tomorrow we will have a party to celebrate. I shall invite you and your mama and Mr. and Mrs. Botts." Mrs. K. felt so happy, she even decided to invite Mr. Wickett.

"Even though you are a cross person," she said to him, "I suppose you were right. A rooster shouldn't live in a small pen at the

edge of town. He should live in the country where nobody will care if he crows at the sun."

Mr. Wickett was a little embarrassed to come to Mrs. K.'s party, but he was too lonely to say no. He came with a box of candy and said, "I'm sorry I gave you so much trouble."

But Mrs. K. told him he shouldn't be sorry. "Life needs a little stirring up now and then," she said. "Besides," she added, "now both Mr. Lincoln and I have found new friends."

Miyo and her mother brought a cake with Mr. Lincoln's name on it. Mr. and Mrs. Botts brought Mrs. K. a plant. "Maybe you can talk to it in Japanese now instead of to Mr. Lincoln," Mrs. Botts said. "And don't worry, I'll take good care of him."

"You come on out to visit us and your rooster any time you like," Mr. Botts added.

Miyo's mother promised that one day soon she would drive them all up to Far Creek. Then they could see how Mr. Lincoln liked his new home.

When the party was over, Mr. Botts carried Mr. Lincoln in a box to the car. Mr. Lincoln gave a squawk of farewell. Mrs. K. promised she would come visit him soon.

"Good-by, Mr. Lincoln. Good-by, Mr. and Mrs. Botts," Miyo called.

From the kitchen, Hamilton, the parrot, screeched. "Good-by, Mr. Lincoln — Good-by."

Jefferson came outside to wag his tail at everybody. Leonardo rubbed up against Mrs. K.'s leg to remind her that he was still there.

Then Mr. Botts honked his horn, and they were gone.

"I hope we'll see each other again soon," Mr. Wickett said to Mrs. K.

"Good night, Mr. Wickett," she answered. "I'm sure we will."

Miyo and her mother thanked Mrs. K. for the nice party and went home. Mrs. K. would say "good night" to her potatoes and onions before going inside.

"Do you think Mrs. K. will miss Mr. Lincoln a lot?" Miyo asked.

"She will for a while," Mother answered, "but now she has a new friend and neighbor to talk to."

Miyo nodded. That was true. She was glad everything had turned out so well. Miyo went to bed feeling good inside.

"Good night, Mama," she called softly.

"Good night, Miyo," Mother answered.

Then, one by one, the lights went out in all the houses along the street. Soon, only the sounds of insects filled the dark night air.

BUTTERFLY WINGS

How would it be
on a day in June
to open your eyes
in a dark cocoon,

And soften one end
and crawl outside,
and find you had wings
to open wide,

And find you could fly
to a bush or tree
or float on the air
like a boat at sea...

How would it be?

—Aileen Fisher

63

Hot Enough for You?

Elizabeth Levy

Part One
The Hydrant

Erica lay in her bed. She felt all sticky. She looked at the clock. Seven-thirty.

"Wow," thought Erica. "If it's this hot at seven-thirty in the morning, it's going to be awful by noon." It was the first heat wave of the summer.

Erica got up. Her father was in the kitchen. "Hot enough for you, Erica?" he asked, as he sat down to read the paper.

Before Erica could answer, her older brother Jay came into the room.

"Hot enough for you, Dad?" he asked.

Their father shook his head yes, and kept reading the paper.

Next their mother hurried in, for she was late for work. "Hot enough for every-body?" she asked. She gave Erica and Jay a quick kiss and was gone. Their father left for work a few minutes later.

Erica got her breakfast and looked out the window. Already the street was filled with people. It was too hot to stay inside the apartment. But Erica knew that soon the street would be just as hot.

"Do you want to go outside?" asked Jay.

"I guess so," said Erica. "What do you want to do today?"

"It's too hot to do anything," said Jay. And he was right. It was 95°.

Erica and Jay sat on the steps in front of their apartment. Everyone who went by asked, "Hot enough for you?"

"Nobody ever waits for you to answer," thought Erica. "It's such a silly question, *'Hot enough for you...hot enough for you?'*"

Just then their friend Susan came over. "Hot enough for you?" she asked.

66

"It's more than hot enough for me!" shouted Erica. *"It's much too hot for me."*

"I think the heat's got to her," said Jay.

"Let's do something about the heat. Let's not just talk about it," said Erica.

"What?" asked Jay and Susan.

"I don't know," said Erica. "But there has to be something we can do."

Finally, they decided to go for a walk. They got up and walked slowly down the street.

The air seemed to get hotter with every step they took. Finally, Jay stopped. "This is no good," he said. "Walking isn't the way to cool off."

They turned around and walked slowly back toward the apartment. Erica looked down at the sidewalk as she walked. Suddenly she yelled, "Look! There's water!"

"Where?" said Susan.

"In the gutter," said Erica. "I wonder where it's coming from?" She began following the stream of water beside the curb. Jay and Susan followed her.

As they turned the corner, they saw that the water was coming from a fire hydrant. Someone had taken off the cap. Water was pouring out in a hard, steady stream.

"Great!" said Jay. "Now we can cool off!"

They ran to the hydrant. But the water was coming out full blast. The pressure was so strong that it made them fall right off the curb into the gutter.

"Well, at least we're cool," said Erica, picking herself up out of the gutter.

"If only so much water weren't being wasted," sighed Susan.

"The way it is now," said Jay, "you could get hurt trying to play in it."

Erica sat with her toes in the gutter. She stared at the stream of water for a long time.

Part Two
Erica the Inventor

"You know," Erica said at last, "if we could put something with holes in it over the hydrant, the water wouldn't be so strong. We could play in it, and it wouldn't hurt."

"Like what?" asked Susan.

Erica looked around. She couldn't think of anything that would work. Then she saw a top of a garbage can. It was being thrown out. She ran to get it.

"Look," explained Erica, "if we made holes in the garbage can top and somehow got it on the hydrant, it would work!"

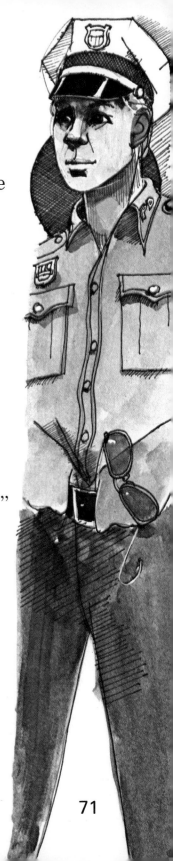

"Well," said Jay, "it can't hurt to try."

They got some tools and made holes all over the garbage can top. Then they tried to fit it over the water. But the pressure of the water was so strong that the top kept flying out of their hands.

They were trying it for about the fifth time when a police officer came over and asked, "What's going on here?"

"We didn't open the hydrant," said Jay. "Somebody else did. We just found it open."

"I believe you," said the police officer.

"You're not strong enough to open the hydrant. But what are you doing with that garbage can top?"

"We were trying to make a sprinkler," said Erica. She took the garbage can top and explained to the police officer how it would work.

"You're quite an inventor," said the police officer, as he put the cap back on the hydrant.

"We have to keep these caps on," he said. "The city loses too much water when the hydrants are open. If there were a fire, there might not be enough pressure to put it out. I wish we could have sprinklers though. It's a good way to cool off. Well, stay out of trouble."

He handed the garbage can top back to Erica and went down the street.

The heat wave went on all week. Erica, Susan, and Jay were miserable, as was everyone else in the city.

Then one day, when they were sitting on the steps in front of their apartment, the police officer came by again.

"Where's the inventor?" he asked.

Erica jumped up.

"I've been looking for you," said the police officer. "There's a surprise waiting for you at the police station."

"What kind of surprise?" asked Jay.

"Come with me and you'll see," said the police officer.

At the police station there were lots of people standing around with television cameras.

"I've found her! I've found the inventor!" said the police officer.

Erica looked up and saw a man she knew was the mayor. She couldn't imagine what was going on.

The mayor cleared his throat and began to talk.

"I have something important to say. It's something very nice for all the children of our great city." He stopped and smiled for the television cameras.

"Everyone knows we are having a very bad heat wave," the mayor went on to say. "Some people have opened fire hydrants, but that is very dangerous."

"As of today," said the mayor, "we are going to put sprinkler caps on the hydrants whenever we have a heat wave. The sprinklers will save most of the water, yet the children will still be able to cool off. The little girl who thought up the idea is here beside me. And we are going to put the first sprinkler cap on her block."

Erica was still not sure what was happening.

The mayor and the police officer took her hands. With the cameras following, they walked up the street to the fire hydrant in front of Erica and Jay's house.

"I told your idea to a friend of mine," whispered the police officer. "And my friend took the idea to the mayor. The mayor liked the idea, and now there are going to be sprinklers all over the city."

Then the mayor gave the go-ahead. Two police officers placed a shining new sprinkler cap on the fire hydrant.

"And now," said the mayor, "Erica, the inventor of the fire hydrant sprinkler, her brother, and her friend Susan will show everyone how this wonderful new sprinkler works."

Susan, Jay, and Erica took off their shoes and played in the soft spray. They got all wet and cool.

It looked like so much fun that the mayor decided to take his shoes off and play in the water, too. The police officer did the same thing.

Soon everyone was very wet and very happy, but no one was quite as happy as Erica.

Margarita's Gift

Ann Devendorf

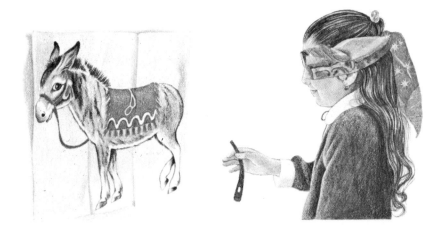

Margarita was at Barbara's birthday party. Margarita felt a little out of place because she didn't speak English very well. She had just moved to the United States from Mexico.

Margarita wasn't very good at the games either. When they played pin-the-tail-on-the-donkey, Margarita pinned the tail right on the tip of one of the donkey's ears! The winner of the game opened her prize. It was a tiny straw horse.

"I bought all the prizes for the party across the border in Mexico," said Barbara to Margarita. "I like to shop in Mexico."

"I do, too," said Margarita. "It's easier for me to shop in Mexico. I speak better Spanish than English."

The next game was guessing the number of beans in a jar. Margarita didn't even come close. She guessed 77, and there were 139 beans in the jar! The winner of the guessing game got six Mexican jumping beans for a prize.

"Hold them in your hand and warm them up," said Barbara to the winner. "Then the beans will begin to jump."

For the last game, they tried to hit a *piñata*. The *piñata* was made in the shape of a horse. It hung on a long rope. The *piñata* could be moved up or down by tugging on the rope.

Margarita knew that the inside of the horse was filled with candies. When the horse was broken, the candies would tumble out.

Margarita watched as each child put on a blindfold and swung at the *piñata* with the handle of a broom. Some of the children hit the horse with glancing blows. Barbara pulled on the rope and made the horse dance away from the swinging broom handle.

Margarita thought, "I know I can hit that *piñata*. I've had practice with *piñatas* many times. I know I must hit above where I last see the horse, because Barbara will pull the horse upward."

Margarita was last. As she was putting on the blindfold, she thought, "I don't want to smash the horse. I know Barbara would like to keep it and hang it in her room."

Margarita brought the broomstick back and swung. She missed. She missed on purpose.

"Oh," sighed Barbara, "I'm so glad my horse isn't smashed." She turned the horse upside down and the candies tumbled from a hole in the top.

Barbara's mother called the children to the table for cake and ice cream. Barbara blew out all the candles on the cake. Margarita enjoyed the cake and ice cream. But she found it difficult to chatter in English with the other children at the table. She felt quite alone.

Then Barbara's mother brought in a huge plate of fortune cookies and put them on the table.

"Oh, good! Fortune cookies!" shouted the children. Their eyes sparkled.

"We got the fortune cookies in Mexico, too," said Barbara.

"I hope I get a good fortune," said one of the children.

"So do I," said another.

Each child carefully picked a fortune cookie from the plate. They cracked them open, and then they groaned.

"The fortunes are written in Spanish!" they exclaimed. "We can't read them!"

"Oh," sighed Barbara. "I never thought about that when I bought them."

"Neither did I," said Barbara's mother. "I should have realized the fortunes would be written in Spanish!"

"I'm so disappointed," said Barbara.

"Don't be," said Margarita. "I can read the fortunes. I'll be happy to do so."

"Read mine!" called a child.

"And mine, too!" called another.

All the children crowded around Margarita. She read their fortunes and translated them into English. The children laughed and giggled. Margarita did, too.

"I'm so glad you can read Spanish," said Barbara.

"We all are," the children agreed.

Margarita felt happy inside. She peeked again at her fortune. It read: "*Su futuro sera muy contento.*" This means, "Your future will be very happy."

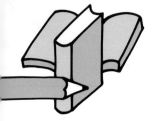

What's the Meaning of This?

Some words look alike and sound alike. But they have different meanings. You have to read how the word is used in a sentence. Then you can find out what it means.

> I went to the <u>bank</u> to get some money.
> We often sit on the <u>bank</u> of the river.

In the first sentence, *bank* means "a place where people keep their money." In the second sentence, *bank* means "the land on the side of a river or stream."

Read each set of meanings. Then read the numbered sentences. Choose the right meaning for each sentence. Then write that meaning on your paper.

Set A
To <u>play</u> is to have fun.
A <u>play</u> is a story that people act out.

1. We're doing a <u>play</u> about Abe Lincoln.
   1. A <u>play</u> is a story that people act out.

2. Gordon wants to <u>play</u> all day.

3. The <u>play</u> will begin at seven o'clock.

Set B

A <u>ring</u> is the sound of a bell.

A <u>ring</u> is a band someone wears on a finger.

1. I lost my <u>ring</u> in the ocean.

2. We heard the <u>ring</u> of a bell.

Set C

A <u>watch</u> is a small timepiece that is often worn on the arm.

To <u>watch</u> is to look at something closely and carefully.

1. Allison broke her <u>watch</u> while playing.

2. Please <u>watch</u> the baby until I get back.

Set D

A <u>tip</u> is the end of something.

A <u>tip</u> is money given to someone for doing a job well.

1. We left a large <u>tip</u> in the restaurant after a fine meal.

2. The <u>tip</u> of the mountain was in a cloud.

Harlequin
and The Gift of Many Colors

Adapted from a story by Remy Charlip and Burton Supree

Paintings by Remy Charlip

Part One

Only a Blanket

Harlequin awoke. His room was dark. The stars and the moon were still in the sky. It was chilly when he got out of bed, so Harlequin wrapped his blanket around him. When he walked to the window, he felt as if he were wearing the night.

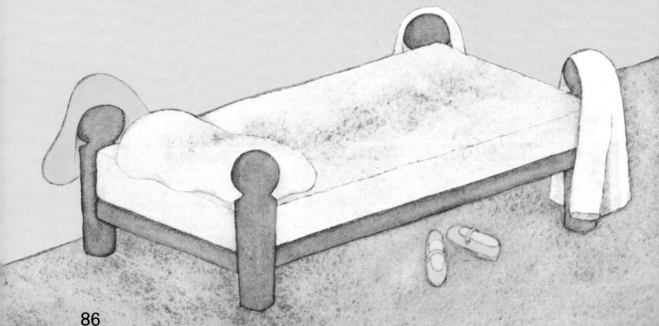

In the dim light, he saw people passing in the street below. They had all left home in the dark to get to the town square early this morning. They were bringing great trays of cakes, pies, and cookies that would be sold tonight. The children were all up helping, too.

But Harlequin sighed. He got back into his warm bed. He pulled the covers over his head.

The children could hardly wait for tonight's great Carnival. There would be games with prizes and candy and ice cream. And there would be dancing and singing and joking with all their friends.

"But where is Harlequin?" one of the children asked, "I haven't seen him all morning."

Harlequin was almost always the first one up, and the one to lead the others in all sorts of fun.

"Maybe he was bad and his mother won't let him come out."

"Maybe he's sick. We'd better go see." And they all ran off to Harlequin's house.

"Harlequin! Harlequin, are you there?" He appeared at the window wearing his blanket.

"Are you all right? Come on out!" His friends all started talking at once.

"Harlequin, the fireworks are all finished."

"My father says I can stay up as late as I want."

"Can you smell the chocolate?"

"Hurry, let's get back to the square."

Slowly Harlequin dressed and came down.

Walking back to the square, the children began
to talk about the best thing of all. Tonight everyone was going to wear a new costume for the first
time. With masks over their faces no one would
know them. Oh, what tricks they would get away
with then!

But it was hard not to brag and tease with little
hints about their costumes.

"Mine is yellow."

"My suit is soft and blue."

"Wait till you see mine. It's the most beautiful
red."

"I've got the biggest green buttons you ever saw." They were all talking at once, parading around in their old clothes, and showing off as if they were already wearing their new ones.

It was only then that they noticed how quiet and gloomy Harlequin had been all this time.

"What are you going to wear tonight, Harlequin?" They all turned to him.

Harlequin didn't say anything.

"Oh, Harlequin, you've got to tell. We told you."

"Well," said Harlequin, thinking fast, "I'll wear my blanket as a cape."

They thought Harlequin was fooling them as he often did.

"Not that old thing!"

"Come on, Harlequin, give us a clue."

"What color is it?"

"What are you going to wear tonight?"

"Nothing," Harlequin answered. "I'm not even coming tonight."

And he turned and ran away.

Harlequin not coming? How could that be? How could he miss Carnival?

Perhaps he was still fooling. He was always playing tricks.

"Wait," one of them said, "I think I know why he's not coming tonight. He doesn't have a new costume."

And it was then that they all understood what was the matter. Harlequin had nothing to wear because his mother was too poor to buy him a costume.

"What can we do? Where can we get him a costume?" they said.

Part Two
A Piece of Cloth

"I know! I have an idea. My coat doesn't need to be so long. I can cut some off and give it to Harlequin. And if we each give him a piece of cloth, then he will have enough for a whole new costume."

"That's true! My dress doesn't need to be so long either."

"Let's go and get our cloth and meet in front of Harlequin's house."

The sun was high when all the children met at Harlequin's house. Each one was carrying a piece of cloth.

When Harlequin answered the knock on the door, he was surprised to see all his friends. Then they held out the pieces of cloth and happily pushed them into his hands.

But when the children saw Harlequin's arms filled with the cut-off bits and scraps, they were sad. Each piece was a different shape and size and color. Some were shiny, some were fuzzy. None of the pieces matched. They looked like a bunch of old rags.

95

Harlequin smiled and thanked them. But the children were afraid they had made him more unhappy by giving him such a useless gift.

"I feel so stupid," one of them whispered.

Unhappily they said good-by and left.

When they were gone, Harlequin stared at the scraps of cloth in his arms.

"What can I do with these?" he thought. "Nothing. Not one piece is big enough for a pant leg or even a sleeve."

He climbed the stairs to his room, thinking that he would not go out again until Carnival was over.

He threw the pieces of cloth into the air. But as the pieces fell to the floor, one piece stuck to his shirt. He looked at it for a moment. And then he had an idea.

When his mother came home, Harlequin told her all that had happened.

Then he told her his idea.

"Do you think if we put all these scraps onto my old suit, it would make a good costume?"

His mother looked at the pieces of cloth. She turned them over and over in her hands. Would it work?

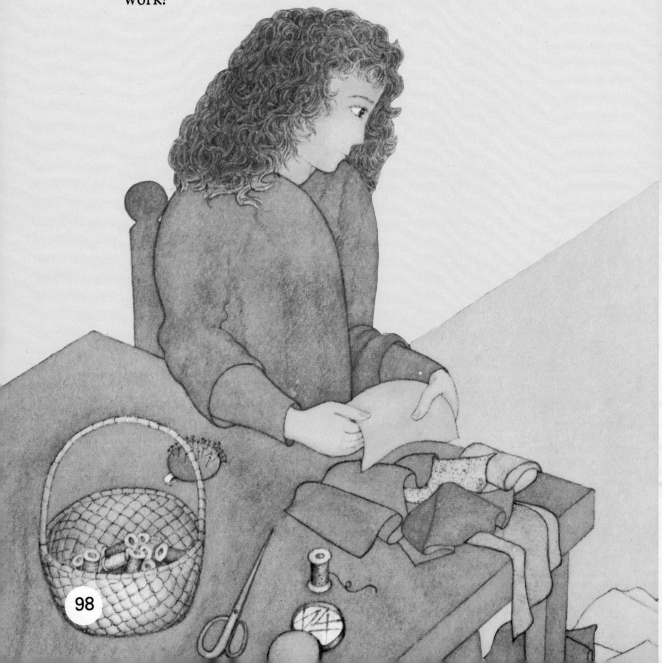

Then she smiled, "I think it would be beautiful."

And they both set to work. Harlequin chose a blue piece. Then he pinned a green one next to it. He pinned all the pieces where he wanted them. His mother began to sew them on.

The sewing took a long time. While his mother was sewing the pieces on his old pants, Harlequin climbed into bed to keep warm. And before he knew it, he had fallen asleep.

But his mother worked on, worried that she might not be able to finish in time.

"Wake up, Harlequin, it's all finished!"

Moonlight streamed into his room. He heard music and shouting far away. He blinked his eyes. For a moment he didn't know where he was.

Then he knew that he was not dreaming. His mother was standing by his bed, smiling. She was holding up a beautiful rainbow-colored suit.

"It's finished!" He threw the covers off and jumped out of bed. "Let me put it on!"

"How wonderful you look!" his mother said proudly. He spun around and around, as bright as a butterfly. "Oh, thank you, I love it," Harlequin said as he put on his mask and his big hat. "It's wonderful!"

And in a moment he ran off to the town square.

The town square was wild with color and noise. All the world seemed to be dancing and singing there. Wonderful smells of cooking meats and sweet pies filled the air. Musicians were playing all the songs everyone liked to hear.

Harlequin's friends had all come early because the first one to come to a booth to buy something did not have to pay. They laughed and joked as they ran from one booth to another, trying to guess who was behind each mask. But they kept looking out for Harlequin, too. They were hoping that by some chance their best friend might be able to come to Carnival.

Suddenly someone appeared in a costume so fantastic that everyone stopped what they were doing. The children all gathered around to see.

"What a splendid costume!"

"I've never seen anything so beautiful!"

"Who is it?"

"Where is he from?"

"Do you know him?" No one knew.

Whoever it was, he began to leap and dance and turn so joyfully that the crowd laughed and clapped with joy. All the many different colors he wore sparkled in the light.

In a flash one of the children noticed a piece of his own costume.

"That piece of blue is mine!" he shouted.

"That shiny red piece is mine!" said another.
"That must be Harlequin!"

"Harlequin! Harlequin!" the children cheered, as
they raced through the crowd. They danced around,
hugging him and each other.

And Harlequin was the happiest of them all on
this happy night, for he was clothed in the love of
his friends.

This painting of Harlequin was done in 1923. It was painted by a very famous artist named Pablo Picasso. Throughout his lifetime Picasso painted many different Harlequins.

Nancy White

Part One
His Younger Years

When Pablo Picasso was a little boy,
he lived in a little town in Spain. Nobody ever asked him what he wanted to
be when he grew up. Everybody knew that
he was already an artist.

His mother liked to tell people that
his first words were, "Piz, piz!" This is
baby talk for *lápiz,* which is the Spanish
word for *pencil.* Stretched out on the floor
with a piece of paper and his pencil,
Pablo drew pictures even before he had
learned to walk. As a very little boy, he
liked crayons and chalk better than any
of his other toys.

Pablo's father, Don José, was an artist. He was very proud of his son. He spent a lot of time teaching the little boy how to draw and paint. Pablo's ability delighted all of his family and their friends.

Using only one line, he could draw a person, an animal, or a bird that looked almost alive. He often played the "Animal Game" with his little sister Lola and his young friends. His big eyes sparkling, he would say to them, "Do you want a little horse? Or a dog? Or a bull?" Then he would quickly cut out a tiny paper animal that was shaped just like a dog, or a horse, or a bull.

Pablo did not like school. All he really wanted to do was draw. He spent many happy hours in his father's studio. He drew pictures of pigeons he saw through the windows. He made many drawings of Lola. He never grew tired of watching his father work or listening to him explain the uses of pencils and chalk and different kinds of paint.

When Pablo was ten years old, things suddenly changed. Don José took a job as an art teacher and Pablo went to his father's school. Besides teaching, Don José painted pictures to be sold. After school he often asked Pablo to help with these paintings. One day Don José went for a walk, leaving Pablo to finish a painting of some pigeons. When he returned, he stood for a long time looking at the finished picture. Pablo waited, watching his father's face.

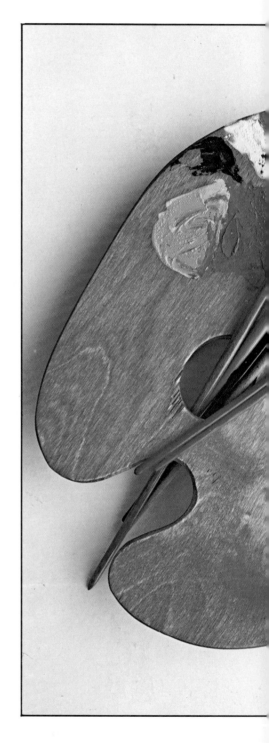

It was very quiet in the studio. Finally, Don José walked over to his work table. He began gathering up his brushes and paint. He put everything in a big box. Then he handed the box to Pablo.

He told Pablo that from now on there would be only one artist in the family. The pigeons in the picture were so real that it seemed as though they might fly away. Don José now knew that Pablo's ability was far greater than his own. He himself would give up painting and spend his time teaching his son.

When Pablo was fourteen, the family moved to Barcelona. Don José began teaching at the School of Fine Arts. Pablo was excited about living in a big city and being near the art school.

Because of Don José, the school decided to let Pablo take the test for the best class. For this test, each artist was given four weeks to finish a drawing. Pablo finished his in one day. And his work was so good that he joined the class at once. During the rest of his life, Pablo kept this ability to work quickly. Some of his best pictures were painted in a very short time.

Part Two
A Very Famous Artist

When Pablo was sixteen, he went to Madrid to study art. But he became very sick and had to leave school. He spent the summer at the home of a friend in the country. Here Pablo had fields, farm animals, and new people to draw.

Returning to Barcelona the following fall, Pablo saw that he would have to make some money by painting and selling some pictures.

Some of Pablo's pictures won prizes. But people wouldn't buy them when they found out the artist was a teenager.

When he was nineteen years old, Pablo decided that he must go to Paris, where he could be with other young artists and writers. In Paris his money did not last very long, and Pablo did not sell many of his pictures.

During these years he was often cold, hungry, and sad. But he kept on painting and painting and painting. The people he saw along the waterfront and on the streets were cold, hungry, and sad, too. He watched them. Then he went home to his tiny studio and painted them. He tried to remember just how they looked, and how they made him feel. These years have become known as his "Blue Period."

During this period, the colors of his pictures were mostly blues, greens, and grays. These colors reflected his sadness and the sadness of the people he painted.

This picture of Harlequin was painted during Picasso's "Blue Period."

Baltimore Museum of Art, Francis B. Mayer

At the age of twenty-three, Picasso moved to Paris for good. At last people began to want his pictures. The next few years are called his "Rose Period." During this period, he painted in happy colors: pinks and reds. This picture was painted during Picasso's "Rose Period."

Picasso later started a type of painting which he thought was more important than anything he had ever done. It is called "Cubism." This picture is a cubist painting.

Pablo Picasso, whose art is loved throughout the world, was one of the most famous artists of all time.

Walter In Love

Alicen White

Walter was in love.

Walter was in love with Tita.

Tita was a beautiful dancer from Spain. She was a Spanish cocker spaniel, proud as well as pretty.

Walter was not proud, but he was handsome. He was an American cocker spaniel.

He was a dog-about-town.

Walter was a happy dog until he saw Tita. Then he got to be moony. He fell madly in love with her. He went to the theater to look at Tita every night for sixty-six nights. Also Wednesday and Saturday afternoons.

He sent her boxes of roses—red roses and white roses, yellow roses and pink roses. He sent her boxes of candy—hard candy and soft candy, coffee candy and peppermint candy. He sent her boxes of beads—gold beads and silver beads, small and large.

He sat by the stage door each night to
see Tita come out after the show. He wore
his best top hat, white tie, and black
tails, of course. But every night she walked
past him with her nose in the air, decked
out in the beads he had sent her. She had
a rose between her teeth, and a box of
candy in her paws. She did not know it
was Walter who was sending her all these
fine things.

You see, Walter was not good at writing. He wrote all the letters backwards. So, of course, he wrote WAƚTƎЯ for "Walter." Tita did not understand this. She could not read the name of her admirer. If you had been Tita, you would have guessed it. But remember, she left school when she was only two. Tita always got the roses and the candy and the beads, because the card on each box was always right. 'TO TITA' it said.

Walter could not write 'TO TITA' the wrong way, because the letters are the same backwards and forwards. Turned around they still spell 'TO TITA.' Lucky for Tita!

119

Well, time went by, and still Tita did not know that Walter loved her. He was too shy to speak to her. All his pocket money went for roses and candy and beads for Tita. He could not eat his dinner. At night, because he could not sleep, he would stare up at the moon. Then he would feel moonier than ever. Walter was so miserable that he made up his mind to write Tita a letter.

He got some lovely paper at the best store in town. He bought a pen with a long feather on it, and this is what he wrote:

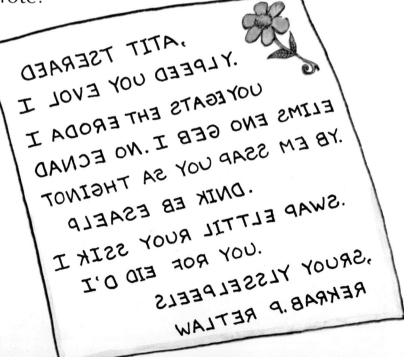

DEAREST TITA,
I LOVE YOU DEARLY.
I ADORE THE STARS YOU
GAZED ON. I BEG NO ONE SMILE
TONIGHT AS YOU PASS ME BY.
PLEASE BE KIND.
I KISS YOUR LITTLE SWAP.
I'D DIE FOR YOU.
RESPECTFULLY YOURS,
WALTER R. BARKER

That night Walter did not send Tita roses or candy or beads. Just the letter. Then he sat shyly in his usual spot outside the theater and hoped.

Tita found the letter on her dressing table after the last dance number. She tore it open but could not read it.

"Is it in French?" she asked her French maid.

"No, madame. It is a Chinese fan letter," said the maid.

"But I do not understand Chinese," said Tita. "So pin it up on the wall beside my Japanese fan letter."

Then she turned her back to the dressing table, took up her looking glass, and began to comb her lovely long ears.

But what did she see reflected in her little mirror through the big one over the dressing table? Walter's letter!

Now it did not look so much like a Chinese fan letter. Tita could read two words in English—'YOU' and 'I'—as well as 'TITA,' of course.

"It is a code and I am going to crack it!" cried Tita, throwing down her comb. She tore Walter's letter down from the wall. Her pretty nose sniffed each word in turn. At the ninth word, 'THƎ,' she stopped and gave a sharp yell.

"That's it! 'THƎ' means 'THE.' It is a well-known English word. How clever I am! The 'E' is turned the wrong way, and so are the other letters. I'll turn them all the right way at once!"

Using her lipstick as a pencil, Tita wrote Walter's letter the right way round on the big dressing table mirror.

This is what it said:

DEAREST TITA,

I LOVE YOU DEEPLY.

I ADORE THE STAGE YOU DANCE ON.

I BEG ONE SMILE TONIGHT AS YOU PASS ME BY. PLEASE BE KIND. I KISS YOUR LITTLE PAWS. I'D DIE FOR YOU.
SLEEPLESSLY YOURS,
WALTER P. BARKER

"Walter! The admirer who sends me boxes and boxes of roses and candy and beads," cried Tita, sticking a red rose behind her ear. "He must be the handsome dog who sits outside in the cold each night to see me step into my car!"

"He must be very rich, madame," sighed Mimi, the French maid.

"I like that," said Tita. "And I like it that he is kind and good and would die for me."

"Maybe," said Mimi.

"I am sure of it!" cried Tita. "I must not keep him waiting one more night."

When she walked out of the stage door, there sat Walter as usual. His eyes were shining full of love.

Then Tita smiled. Her smile lit up the sky for Walter, like the sun and the moon and all the stars.

"Will you marry me, my love?" he asked, softly holding her feathery paw in his.

"I am yours!" whispered the beautiful Spanish spaniel, her face close to his.

Together they walked off to Walter's big car. Walter was a happy dog again. But Tita never told him how near he had come to losing her because of his back-to-front paw-writing.

So he wrote love notes to her that way, quite happily, for the rest of their lives.

Don't tell me
that I talk too much!

Don't tell me that I talk too much!
Don't say it!
Don't you dare!
I only say important things
Like why it's raining where.
Or when or how or why or what
Might happen here or there.
And why a thing is this or that
And who is bound to care.
So don't tell me I talk too much!
Don't say it!
DON'T YOU DARE!

—Arnold Spilka

THE FRIENDSHIP GAME

Dina Anastasio

The first day in any new school is hard. But the first day in a new school where everyone speaks French and you speak English is awful! Just ask Jennifer!

Of course, Mademoiselle Sagan, the third-grade teacher, spoke French *and* English. But no one else did. No one but Jennifer. She spoke a little French.

She could say: *Good morning, Good night, Give me some ice cream, please, Where is the ladies' room?* and a few other things. But she didn't know enough to strike up a friendship with anyone in her class who didn't speak English at all.

Jennifer didn't make any friends. She didn't even make an enemy! No one seemed to know that Jennifer was even there. And, before long, she began to feel a bit like an old shoe.

When her father had first told her about his new job and moving to Paris, Jennifer had been quite excited. And when they had talked about schools, she thought it would be exciting to go to a French school. She would meet new people and she would learn to speak French much faster.

It had all sounded so perfect then. But somehow it hadn't turned out that way. Here she was in a French school, with French children, and no one to talk to.

Since Jennifer was not a quitter, she tried very hard to make the best of it. The other kids weren't really mean to her or anything. They just acted like she wasn't there.

Jennifer sat in the very back of the room. She never said anything in class, since everyone was speaking French. So you can see why everyone forgot that she was there.

That evening her father said, "Well, Jennifer, you'll just have to learn to speak French right away." And her mother said, "That's right, dear. The other children aren't going to learn English, so you'll just have to try harder to learn French."

So Jennifer tried harder. She learned to say: *Do you have any hot dogs?* and *Boy, is it hot in here!* and *The rocket crash-landed!* and a few other things. But her life didn't get any easier. She still didn't make any friends.

The loneliest time of Jennifer's day was always recess. The other children played games that she didn't know. They would have been easy enough to learn had Jennifer known how to speak French. But since she didn't, she had to spend each recess alone for a long time.

One day, the other children were playing a game that looked something like tag. Jennifer went inside and asked Mademoiselle Sagan for a piece of chalk. With it she drew a hopscotch game on the sidewalk and started to play by herself. It was no fun alone, so she pretended that she was playing with a friend. This way she had someone to play with, and yet she always won the game. For the first time in a long time, Jennifer began to have a little fun.

Jennifer played hopscotch at recess for about a week before she began to get bored with it.

"It needs something!" Jennifer whispered to her imaginary friend. Then with her chalk, she wrote out the words for the numbers. The game now looked like this:

It wasn't very different, but it made her feel a little more at home.

Whenever Jennifer and her imaginary friend played hopscotch, they said the numbers out loud as they jumped. Life was beginning to look a lot better for Jennifer.

Then one day, Jennifer noticed that a girl in her class was watching her. Her name was Mimi. All of the other girls seemed to like her very much.

"She must think we're crazy," Jennifer whispered to her imaginary friend. And she quickly stopped counting.

The next day, when Jennifer was playing, Mimi walked over and watched her very carefully.

Jennifer said "hello" in French, and Mimi said the same. But they didn't say anything else. *The rocket crash-landed!* or *Where is the ladies' room?* would have sounded pretty silly. Jennifer still didn't know how to say, *Do you want to play?* or *Nice day, isn't it?* or anything like that. And so they just stood there, smiling at each other. Jennifer felt very foolish.

Suddenly Mimi leaned down. She picked up the piece of chalk and began to write on Jennifer's hopscotch game. When she was through, the game looked like this:

Then Mimi picked up a stone, threw it on the number "one," and began to play. As she jumped, she pronounced the French numbers that she had written, very carefully. When she was done, she pointed to the game and said "you go," in English.

Jennifer threw her stone on "one" and began to hop. As she hopped onto each square, she said the number in French.

When she was finished, Mimi cried "oui, oui," (which is French for *yes, yes)*. Jennifer began to play again, but this time she said the numbers in English as she jumped. She was very careful in pronouncing them very clearly.

Next Mimi played, saying the numbers in English. When they had learned to pronounce the words perfectly, they played a real game. As they hopped from square to square, Jennifer said the words in French. Mimi said them in English. Mimi won, but Jennifer didn't mind. She thought she might have a friend at last. And she had learned eight new French words.

137

Mimi didn't speak to Jennifer for the rest of the day, but she smiled at her every so often. Jennifer was very happy.

The next day at recess Mimi and Jennifer played their game again. Jennifer won four games. Mimi won two. By the time they were through, they each knew their numbers very well. They couldn't wait until that evening to tell their families.

That night it rained. The next day when Jennifer and Mimi came out for recess, their game was almost gone.

Jennifer ran inside and got another piece of chalk. Then she began to draw. When she was through, the game looked like this:

When Mimi saw what Jennifer had drawn, she began to smile. Then she took the chalk and wrote the words in French, so that the game looked like this:

Then she pronounced the words carefully so that Jennifer could learn them.

Jennifer did the same with the English words. Before long the girls were able to pronounce the words perfectly in English and French.

Then they began to play. Jennifer won the first game, and then it was time to go inside.

Throughout the fall, Jennifer worked very hard to learn to speak French. And Mimi, having found that learning English can be fun, worked even harder.

By the time winter came to Paris, Jennifer and Mimi had learned about a hundred new words by playing hopscotch. So they were able to speak to each other. Their words were sometimes in English and sometimes in French, but they each knew what the other meant——and that was all that mattered.

The River Is a Piece of Sky

From the top of a bridge
The river below
Is a piece of sky—
    Until you throw
    A penny in
    Or a cockle shell
    Or a pebble or two
    Or a cobblestone
    Or a fat man's cane—
And then you can see
It's a river again.

The difference you'll see
When you drop your penny:
The river has splashes.
The sky hasn't any.

—John Ciardi

The Girl Who Found a Dragon

Darlene Geis

Mary Anning lived in an English seaside village. Her father used to hunt for fossil shells, which he sold to the summer visitors. From the time Mary was five years old, her father used to take her with him. There were many fossils to be found on the cliffs and beaches outside the town.

When Mary was ten years old, her father died. But she carried on the hard and dangerous work herself. She was only a child but she knew a lot about fossils.

Then one day in 1811, when she was only twelve years old, Mary Anning made one of the great discoveries of her time. She found her first "dragon." It was a skeleton of fossil bones in a blue slate layer of the cliff. There it lay, almost seven feet long!

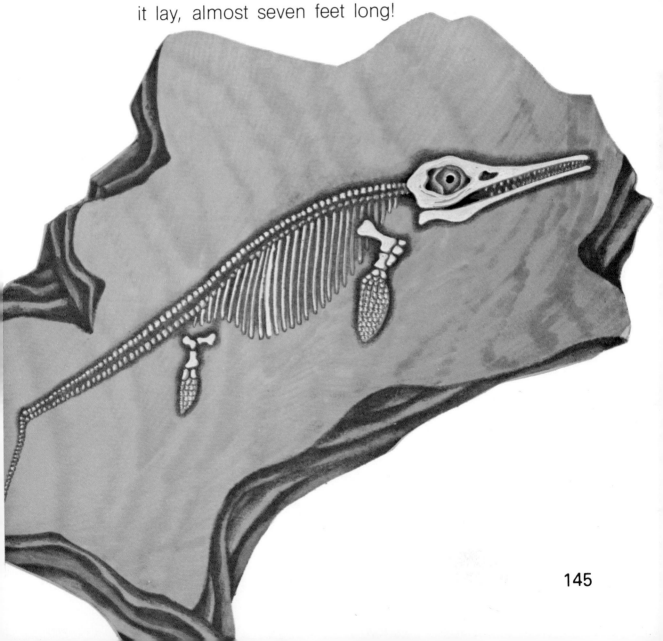

Some men from the village helped Mary pry the stone loose from the cliff. She saw at once that her dragon was not just something to be sold to the summer people. So she had it taken to a very important man. He paid her more than one hundred dollars for it.

He sent it to a museum. Scientists from all over the world studied the fossil dragon. Mary Anning collected fossils for scientists from then on. Once a king even came to her shop and bought a fossil from her.

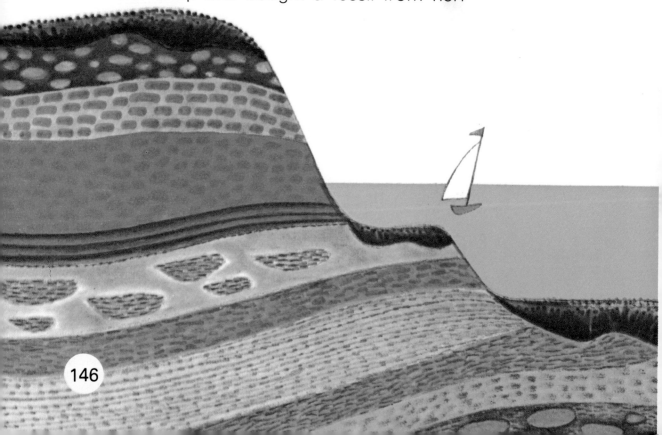

Mary learned about the different rock layers in the cliff, too. She learned which ones might hold the fossils she wanted. Later, she found the fossil of a kind of sea snake. Then some years after that, Mary made her third great discovery. It was the skeleton of a flying reptile. It was the first to be found in England.

Scientists all over the world knew of Mary's work. They were very excited about her fossils. When Mary first found the skeleton of the dragon in the cliffs near her home, she had no idea what it was. Even the scientists knew little about the creature.

In fact, the scientists studied it for seven years before naming it. It seemed to be half fish and half lizard. Finally, the scientists put together the Greek names for fish and lizard. They made the name *ichthyosaur.* Over the years, they have come to understand the story of the reptile. The reptile had crawled back into the sea and become almost like a large fish.

Mary Anning's dragon was a puzzle to scientists, because only the skeleton was there. The skeleton looked like a lizard with a long thin tail (which seemed to be broken and bent near the end). It had a long snout with hundreds of teeth and very large eyes. It had two large front paddles and two tiny rear ones. The scientists tried to find out what the dragon must have looked like. They drew a shape around its bones. It turned out to look very much like a lizard.

Then a very famous scientist became excited about the drawing. He noticed those large front paddles. "Very like a whale," he thought. But whales have no back paddles at all. Instead, they have a very large tail fin with which they move through the water. Their large paddles are only for steering.

The scientist decided that a creature the size of the ichthyosaur must have had a tail fin, too. But since fins have no bones, they would not show up in a skeleton. He guessed that the tail fin would have had strong muscles linking it to the backbone. Such bones always have marks to show where muscles were attached to them.

Sure enough, the ichthyosaur bones had such marks. So the long lizard-like tail bone had really had a large fin attached to it. The fossil backbone had not been broken or bent. It grew down at the end to hold the bottom fin. Now the ichthyosaur was beginning to look more like a fish.

Some years later, another scientist was working on an ichthyosaur skeleton that was in a piece of slate. In order to get at the old bones, the slate had to be chipped and pried off very carefully.

While this scientist was working on the skeleton, he upset a glass of water on the piece of slate. When the water dried, it left a dark shape around the bones that looked like a giant fish! There it was, a beautiful creature, with the long snout, a big tail fin, and—most surprising of all—a sail-shaped fin on top to its back.

That is how, through hard work and a bit of luck, scientists found out what the dragon really looked like. It had been a great puzzle. No one could have guessed how closely this reptile had come to look like a fish because of living a fish's life.

Later ichthyosaur skeletons showed that the mother hatched her eggs inside her body. The baby ichthyosaurs were born alive. Little by little, the whole wonderful story of this water monster was pried from the rocks.

FAMOUS

from *The Guinness Book of World Records*

HERE ARE SOME WORLD RECORDS, JUST WAITING TO BE BROKEN!

TREE CLIMBING

The record for climbing a tree is held by a woman. She climbed a ninety-foot pine tree in thirty-six seconds.

TALKING

Someone talked without stopping for six days and four minutes!

CLAPPING

Two teenagers hold the record for clapping. They clapped, without stopping, for more than fifty-eight hours.

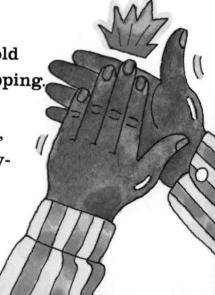

152

FIRSTS

STONE SKIPPING

A person made a stone skip across water twenty-four times with just one throw!

ROLLER COASTING

The record for roller coasting is held by three people. They stayed on a roller coaster for 100 hours. They covered 1,411.2 miles.

WALKING ON HANDS

A man once walked 871 miles on his hands. He walked ten hours a day for fifty-five days.

153

Watch Out!

Some words look alike because they are spelled alike. But these words may not sound alike or have the same meaning. You have to read how the word is used in a sentence. Then you will know how to say the word, and you will know what it means.

Roberto's birthday <u>present</u> is a new bike.
We will <u>present</u> a play about Abe Lincoln.

In the first sentence, *present* means "a gift someone gives to someone else." In the second sentence, *present* means "to show something or someone."

Read each set of word meanings. Then read each numbered sentence. Choose the right meaning for each underlined word. Write that meaning on your paper.

Set A
To <u>bow</u> is to bend your body forward.
A <u>bow</u> is a piece of cloth tied in loops.

1. She put a large blue <u>bow</u> on the present.
   1. A bow is a piece of cloth tied in loops.
2. You should <u>bow</u> to the queen.
3. His apron had a <u>bow</u> at the back.

Set B
The <u>wind</u> is air moving quickly.
To <u>wind</u> is to wrap something in the shape
of a circle.
   1. <u>Wind</u> up the rope when you have finished using it.
   2. The <u>wind</u> blew the nest out of the tree.

Set C
A <u>desert</u> is land with hardly any water.
To <u>desert</u> is to leave someone or something.
   1. The sailors did not <u>desert</u> the ship.
   2. Only a few plants can live in a <u>desert</u>.

Set D
To be <u>close</u> is to be very near something.
To <u>close</u> is to shut something.
   1. A big spider sat much too <u>close</u> to me.
   2. It's very cold, so let's <u>close</u> the door.

Simon Boom Gives A Wedding

Yuri Suhl

Part One

Only the Best

Once there was a man named Simon Boom who liked to brag: "I buy only the best." It didn't matter if the best was a size too short, or a size too long, or altogether out of season. If it was the best, Simon Boom bought it.

One summer day Simon Boom walked into a hat store. He said to the storekeeper, "Give me the best hat you have."

"Very well," said the storekeeper. He brought out the best straw hat in the store.

"Is this the best you have?" said Simon Boom.

"I have a still better hat," said the store-keeper. "But it's made of felt."

"I don't want a better hat," Simon Boom said. "I want the best hat."

"Very well," said the storekeeper. "The very best hat I have is made of wool. It will keep your head warm on the coldest day."

"If it is the very best, I'll buy it," said Simon Boom. And he did.

That summer all the people in town felt cool in their light hats. Only Simon Boom was hot in his heavy winter hat.

"My head feels so warm," thought Simon Boom. "I'll buy myself an umbrella to hide it from the sun." And so he walked into an umbrella store. He said to the storekeeper, "Give me the best umbrella you have."

"Beach umbrella, or rain umbrella?" the storekeeper asked.

"Best umbrella," said Simon Boom.

"Very well," said the storekeeper. She pulled a black umbrella out of the umbrella stand and opened it up. "This is the best I have," she said. "It's very strong. If it doesn't keep the rain off of you, your money will be returned at once."

"If it's the best, I'll buy it," said Simon Boom. And he did.

Now Simon Boom was the only person in town wearing a winter hat and carrying an open rain umbrella on a bright summer day.

158

The umbrella didn't help much and Simon
Boom thought, "I'll buy myself a light suit
to keep cool." And so he walked into a
clothing store. He said to the storekeeper,
"Give me the best suit you have."

"What kind would you like?" asked the
storekeeper.

"The best," Simon Boom answered.

"Very well," said the storekeeper. He brought out a fine tweed suit. "This is made of the finest wool. It will keep you warm on the coldest day. But it may be a little too large for you. What size do you wear?"

"I wear a 38 short," said Simon Boom.

"This suit is a 42 long," the storekeeper said. "And it's the only one left. I'm sorry."

"If it's the best, I'll buy it," Simon Boom said. And he did.

Now Simon Boom was the only person in town wearing a warm winter hat, a warm winter suit, and carrying an open umbrella on a bright summer day.

Simon Boom had a daughter named Rosalie. The time came for Rosalie to get married. Simon Boom said to his wife, "Our daughter is starting out on a new life. I am going to give her the best wedding party ever held in this town. I'll ask the best people and serve the best food. It will be a wedding party the whole town will talk about. I want nothing but the best for my daughter, Rosalie."

"What shall we serve our guests," his wife asked, "fish or chicken?"

"Fish," said Simon Boom. "All kinds of fish. Bluefish, whitefish, cod, and lots more."

Three days before the wedding Simon Boom went to see the fish dealer. "I will need two hundred pounds of the very best fish for my daughter's wedding," he said to the fish dealer. "All kinds of fish."

"Very well," said the fish dealer. "You shall have all the fish you want."

"But I want the best fish," Simon Boom said.

"Our fish are as sweet as sugar," said the fish dealer.

"Did you say sweet as sugar?" Simon Boom asked.

"Upon my word, sir," the fish dealer said. "Sweet as sugar."

"Aha," thought Simon Boom to himself. "If he said sweet as sugar, then sugar must be better than fish. I shall get sugar instead." And so he said to the fish dealer, "I have changed my mind," and he left.

Simon Boom went straight to the sugar merchant. He said, "I will need two hundred pounds of sugar for my daughter's wedding."

"Very well, sir," said the sugar merchant. "You shall have all the sugar you want."

"But I want the very *best* sugar," Simon Boom told the man.

"Our sugar is as sweet as honey," said the sugar merchant.

"Did you say sweet as honey?" Simon Boom asked.

"Upon my word, sir," the sugar merchant said, "sweet as honey"

"Aha," Simon Boom thought to himself. "If he said sweet as honey, then honey must be better than sugar. I shall get honey instead." And so he said to the sugar merchant, "I have changed my mind," and walked away.

Simon Boom went straight to the honey merchant. He said, "I want two hundred jars of honey for my daughter's wedding."

"Very well," said the honey merchant, "You shall have all the honey you want."

"But I want the very *best* honey you have," Simon Boom said.

"Our honey is as clear as oil," said the honey merchant.

"Did you say clear as oil?" Simon Boom asked.

"Upon my word, sir," said the honey merchant, "clear as oil."

"Aha," Simon Boom thought to himself. "If she said clear as oil, then oil must be better than honey. I shall get oil instead." And so he said to the honey merchant, "I have changed my mind," and he left.

Simon Boom then went straight to the oil merchant. He said, "I want two hundred quarts of oil for my daughter's wedding."

"Very well, sir," said the oil merchant. "You shall have all the oil you want."

"But I want the very *best* oil," Simon Boom said.

"Our oil is as pure as spring water," said the oil merchant.

"Did you say pure as spring water?" Simon Boom asked.

"Upon my word, sir," the oil merchant said, "as pure as spring water."

"Aha," Simon Boom thought to himself. "If he said as pure as spring water, then spring water must be better than oil. I shall get spring water instead." And so he said to the oil merchant, "I have changed my mind," and he left.

Part Two

The Very Best

Simon Boom walked all over town looking for a spring-water store. He couldn't find one. He was about to give up when he saw the water carrier. He had two wooden cans of water hanging from the yoke on his back. "Maybe he would know," Simon Boom thought to himself. "He deals in water." And so he ran up to the water carrier and said, "Could you please tell me where I can buy some spring water?"

"Of course I can," said the water carrier, putting his two cans down on the ground.

"At last!" said Simon Boom, feeling much happier now. "I have been looking for that spring-water store all over town and couldn't find it."

"No wonder!" said the water carrier. "The water you are looking for is not in a store. It's in a well."

"But I want spring water," said Simon Boom, "not well water."

"My dear sir," said the water carrier, "well water is the purest, coolest spring water there is."

"Is it also the *best*?" Simon Boom asked.

"The very best," said the water carrier.

"If it is the very best," said Simon Boom, "then I want twenty barrels of it for my daughter's wedding."

"You shall have all the well water you want," said the water carrier. "When is the wedding taking place?"

"In three days," said Simon Boom.

"I'll bring it over just before the guests arrive so the water will be fresh and cool," the water carrier told Simon Boom.

When Simon Boom came home, his wife said, "You look happy. That means you got the fish you wanted."

"Not fish and not sugar either," said Simon Boom.

"You bought chicken instead?"

"Not chicken and not honey either," said Simon Boom.

"You bought meat instead?"

"Not meat and not oil either," Simon Boom said.

"Then what **did** you buy?" his wife wanted to know.

"I bought something that is sweeter than sugar, clearer than honey, purer than oil, and better than all three of them."

"Doesn't it have a name?" his wife asked.

"It has," said Simon Boom. "The Best."

"The best what?"

"That, my dear wife, I want to be a surprise even to you," said Simon Boom.

"But will it come in time for me to cook it?" his wife asked.

"It doesn't have to be cooked," Simon Boom said.

"It doesn't have to be cooked? My, that **is** a surprise."

"It's the Best," said Simon Boom, smiling happily.

A few hours before the wedding party was to begin, Mrs. Boom ordered the servants to set the table. Simon Boom walked into the dining room and saw what they were doing. He shouted to the servants, "Off with the plates! Off with the forks! Off with the spoons! Only the glasses will stay!"

171

Just then Simon Boom's wife walked into the dining room. When she saw what was happening, she was very upset. "I ordered the table set," she told the servants.

"And I ordered it unset," Simon Boom told her. "For my special dish all we need is glasses."

"Not even plates, and forks, and spoons?" his wife said. "This **is** a surprise!"

"The Best," said Simon Boom, smiling happily again.

The water carrier kept his promise. Shortly before the guests began to arrive, he rolled the twenty barrels of well water up the hill to Simon Boom's house. As soon as Rosalie was married, Simon Boom ordered the servants to fill every pitcher in the house with water from the barrels. Then the pitchers were placed all around the table.

It was a warm evening. As soon as the guests arrived, they filled their glasses and drank. "Ah," they said, "fresh, cold water! That's just what we need."

"See how they love it?" said Simon Boom to his wife. "That's because we are serving the Best! The very Best." And he ordered the servants to keep the pitchers full.

Soon the musicians struck up a happy wedding tune. The guests began to dance. When the dance was over, the guests were warm and ready for something to drink.

They went back to the table for some fresh, cold water. Simon Boom watched them fill up their glasses. He said to his wife, "You see what happens when you serve the Best? They love it."

Now the guests were beginning to get hungry. They waited for food. But all they got was more water. They filled their glasses and drank it. "Look how they drink it!" said Simon Boom to his wife. "They just don't seem to get enough of that wonderful well water."

The musicians struck up another lively tune. But the guests were now too hungry to get up and dance. So they sat at the table. They drank some more water to keep their stomachs from rumbling. "Our guests must be pretty hungry by now," said Mrs. Boom to her husband. "All we have been giving them is water. Don't you think we should give them something to eat, too?"

"Of course not!" said Simon Boom. "We are serving the Best, and there is nothing better than the Best."

By twelve o'clock the guests were so full of water that they couldn't even keep their eyes open. They all fell asleep at the table.

"Maybe if they had some food they might be able to stay awake," said Mrs. Boom.

"What they need is some more of that fresh, cold water to wake them up," said Simon Boom. And he ordered the servants to fill up all the glasses.

"Sorry," said the servants, "but the pitchers are empty."

"Then fill up the pitchers!" Simon Boom shouted loudly.

"Sorry," said the servant, "but the barrels, too, are empty."

"Then fill up the barrels!" Simon Boom ordered the servants. "Roll them down to the well and fill them up. Hurry! Hurry! Hurry!" he shouted.

The guests were awakened by Simon Boom's shouting. They thought that, at last, the food was about to be served.

"I have something to say," Simon Boom said. "I know that you would all like to have some of that fresh, cool well water. And you shall have it! I just sent my servants to the well. They will soon return with twenty more barrels of the same water, the Best."

When the guests heard the news that more water was coming, they all got up and made for the door. In a few minutes they were all gone.

"Now look what you have done!" Mrs. Boom said to her husband. "I'll never live down the shame," she cried. "Won't you **ever** listen to me? Imagine, serving only water at my daughter's wedding party!"

"Only water!" Simon Boom shouted. "But what kind of water? I served them water that is:

sweeter than sugar,
clearer than honey,
purer than oil,
and better than all three of them.
I served them the Best.
The VERY Best!"

Over in the Meadow

Olive A. Wadsworth

Over in the meadow,
In the sand, in the sun,
Lived an old mother-toad
And her little toadie one.
"Wink!" said the mother;
"I wink," said the one.
So she winked and she blinked
In the sand, in the sun.

Over in the meadow,
Where the stream runs blue,
Lived an old mother-fish
And her little fishes two.
"Swim!" said the mother;
"We swim," said the two.
So they swam and they leaped
Where the stream runs blue.

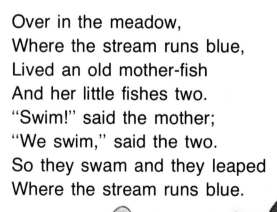

Over in the meadow,
In a hole in a tree,
Lived an old mother-bluebird
And her little birdies three.
"Sing!" said the mother;
"We sing," said the three.
So they sang and were glad
In the hole in the tree.

Over in the meadow,
In the reeds on the shore,
Lived an old mother-muskrat
And her little ratties four.
"Dive!" said the mother;
"We dive," said the four.
So they dived and they burrowed
In the reeds on the shore.

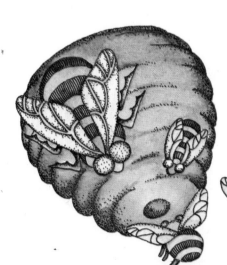

Over in the meadow,
In a snug beehive,
Lived a mother-honeybee
And her little bees five.
"Buzz!" said the mother;
"We buzz," said the five.
So they buzzed and they hummed
In the snug beehive.

179

Over in the meadow,
In a nest built of sticks,
Lived a black mother-crow
And her little crows six.
"Caw!" said the mother;
"We caw," said the six.
So they cawed and they called
In the nest built of sticks.

Over in the meadow,
Where the grass is so even,
Lived a gray mother-cricket
And her little crickets seven.
"Chirp!" said the mother;
"We chirp," said the seven.
So they chirped cheery notes
In the grass soft and even.

Over in the meadow,
By the old mossy gate,
Lived a brown mother-lizard
And her little lizards eight.
"Bask!" said the mother;
"We bask," said the eight.
So they basked in the sun
By the old mossy gate.

Over in the meadow,
Where the clear pools shine,
Lived a green mother-frog
And her little froggies nine.
"Croak!" said the mother;
"We croak," said the nine.
So they croaked and they splashed
Where the clear pools shine.

Over in the meadow,
In a sly little den,
Lived a gray mother-spider
And her little spiders ten.
"Spin!" said the mother;
"We spin," said the ten.
So they spun lace webs
In the sly little den.

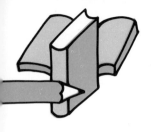

Before and After

Read the lists below.

un- not	**-ful** full of
<u>un</u>real — not real	hope<u>ful</u> — full of hope
re- again	**-er** one who can
<u>re</u>run — run again	dan<u>cer</u> — one who dances

ACTIVITY A Write the words below on your paper. Then write the meaning of each word.

Set 1

   1. redo   1. redo — do again

   2. replace   **3.** reclean   **4.** unlucky

   5. unsafe   **6.** unhappy   **7.** reuse

Set 2

   1. fearful   **2.** teacher   **3.** helpful

   4. painter   **5.** careful   **6.** player

ACTIVITY B Read the sentences on the next page. Look at the underlined word in each sentence. On your paper, write the meaning of the underlined word.

1. It was <u>unfair</u> not to let everyone go.
   1. unfair — not fair
2. The police had to <u>reopen</u> the case.
3. This box of crayons is <u>unused</u>.
4. You need to <u>rebuild</u> your sand castle.
5. The dog was very angry, but Mindy was <u>unafraid</u>.
6. The glass is broken, so we will have to <u>replace</u> it.
7. Please <u>unlock</u> the door and let the cat in.
8. We need a <u>writer</u> for the new book.
9. The music in the restaurant was very <u>restful</u>.
10. Ann's report on animals was very <u>meaningful</u>.
11. Do you think the <u>pitcher</u> is the most important baseball player?
12. Harry is the best <u>jumper</u> in school.
13. On the day of the picnic, we were <u>thankful</u> for the lovely sunshine.
14. The baker made a <u>beautiful</u> wedding cake.

BEGINNINGS

It's not always easy to start doing things in a new way. Sometimes the old way to do something is a good way to do it. Other times, it's just more comfortable not to change. But you should look for better ways to do things.

Thinking About "Beginnings"

1. Why did Mrs. K. have to find something to do about Mr. Lincoln's crowing?
2. How would "Hot Enough for You?" be different if Erica and her friends lived in the country?
3. What gift did Margarita give Barbara?
4. What was special about the cliffs and beaches near Mary Anning's village?
5. Why didn't the way Simon Boom looked for only the best work very well?
6. What better ways can you think of to do some of the things you do?

ENDINGS

There are some problems that are very hard to do anything about. You may even think that you can't do anything about them. But there is always something you can do. Each person must find his or her own way to deal with a problem. Each person's way will be different from that of any other person.

In "Endings," you will read about a boy who has to decide what wish to make. You will read about a mayor who has a problem with a car. As you read, think about how the people deal with their problems. Would you do the same things?

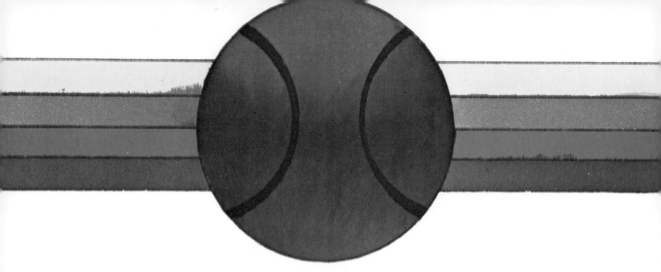

Dr. Naismith's Game

Sally R. Bell

Thump! A soccer ball flew through the air. It landed in a peach basket that hung above the heads of some students and their teacher. The score was 1-0. Dr. James A. Naismith's class had just finished the first game of basketball.

It was December, 1891, in Springfield, Massachusetts. When Dr. Naismith's class arrived, they found two wooden peach baskets hung above the floor. Dr. Naismith explained his new game. There would be two teams. The players would try to throw a soccer ball into the baskets. No one would be allowed to run with the ball.

The students didn't think they'd enjoy this game. But by the time it was half over, they were very excited. When they went home, they told their families and friends about the new game. It was called *basketball*, because it used peach baskets and a soccer ball.

At first, someone had to climb up a ladder to remove the ball from the basket each time a player scored. Within a year, however, someone had invented a new basket. It was made of woven wire. Then the players used poles to push the ball out of the basket.

Finally, someone thought of using rope to make a net. A hole was cut in the bottom of the net. Then the ball fell through the net easily.

There were eighteen students in Dr. Naismith's class. So the first game was played with nine players on a team. For some years, the number of players on a team was decided by how many people wanted to play. One game was played with one hundred players on each team!

Basketball quickly became popular. After only ten years, an organization for basketball was started. The large teams didn't work very well. So one of the first things the new organization did was to make a rule. Only four players were allowed on each team. Later, this rule was changed so that there could be five players on a team.

As basketball became popular, people began to enjoy watching it. They got very excited as they watched their favorite teams. Sometimes they reached out to stop a ball from going into the basket. At last, someone thought of putting a piece of wood behind the basket. Then the people watching the game couldn't reach the basket.

When Dr. Naismith made up his game, he had needed a game that could be played inside. His new game was safe and exciting. It could also be played in a small space. Dr. Naismith had no idea that his invention would become one of the most popular games in the world.

SILLIBILL

William Wiesner

Part One
The Man in the Well

Once upon a time there lived a poor
woman with her only son, whose name
was Sillibill. He was a nice young man,
kind and cheerful, but not very smart.
He loved to play happy songs on his
fiddle or to draw pictures with his
crayons. But he was useless for any
kind of work because he did everything
the wrong way.

One day his mother said, "The pigsty
really needs to be painted. Please, do it
while I do my shopping in town. Use
this red paint."

"Yes, Mother," answered Sillibill. "I'll paint it beautifully." But when she returned in the evening, the pigsty looked as dirty as ever.

"Sillibill," she shouted, "you promised to paint the pigsty."

"Oh, but I did," he answered, and showed her a large piece of board on which he had painted a picture of the pigsty. "Look, I even painted the pig," he added proudly.

"Oh, my poor boy," sighed his mother, "if you only had a little common sense!"

Another time when the mother was sick in bed, she said to her son, "Go and lock the stable door. A thief might get in and steal our new carriage."

"All right," said he, and went into the stable. There, next to the carriage, stood the donkey.

"Hm," thought Sillibill, "a thief can break the lock, but without the donkey, the carriage cannot go anywhere." So he led the donkey behind the house and tied it to the fence. Then he locked the stable door and went to bed.

The next morning the carriage stood where he had left it, but the donkey had been stolen.

"Oh, that poor boy," cried his mother, throwing up her hands. "If he only had a little bit of common sense!"

Another time, when his mother had to leave the house again, she said to Sillibill, "Our soup is on the stove. If you don't watch it, it will boil over, and the whole house will smell awful." But when she came home, she saw thick smoke coming out of the kitchen window. Running in, she found the top of the stove covered with burned soup.

"Oh, Sillibill, why didn't you watch the soup?"

"But, Mother, I watched it all the time. When it boiled over, I opened the window right away to let the smell out."

"Oh, my poor boy," sighed the mother, "this cannot go on. The best thing for you to do is to go out into the wide world to learn some common sense."

"I think you are right, Mother," said Sillibill. He picked up his fiddle, put food and his crayons in his pockets, and set out.

After a while he came to a well where he sat down to eat and drink. But he couldn't find the bucket on the rim of the well. As he bent over the rim, he heard a weak voice calling, "Help, help, I am stuck in the bucket. Please, get me out!"

Sillibill didn't wait even a second. He grabbed the rope and climbed down into the dark hole. There he took hold of the heavy bucket and climbed back, panting and gasping, not stopping once until he had reached the top.

Out of the bucket stepped a little blue man with a long blue beard, who cried, "You are a brave boy, and you have saved my life. But tell me one thing. Why did you take the trouble to climb the rope, when all you had to do was turn the handle to bring the bucket up?"

"Hm," said Sillibill, scratching his head. "I never thought of that."

The little blue man looked carefully at the boy and then said, "I'd like to pay you back for your good deed. I can grant you one wish, but this wish will come true only if you use your common sense. Mind you, I can grant you only ONE. So be careful not to waste it." With these words the little blue man disappeared.

Part Two
The Wish

Sillibill was happy that he now had a free wish. But he decided to wait until he could think of something clever. Since nothing came to his mind, he soon forgot all about the little blue man and his wish.

He walked on until he came to a town that looked very odd. Houses, roofs, doors, windows—all were round. As he walked through the streets, he noticed another strange thing. Wherever he looked, he saw signs with "Don't's."

"Don't... Don't..." The signs went on and on. Sillibill's head was spinning.

Finally, a man hurried by. Sillibill grabbed him by the coattails and asked him, "Good Sir, can you tell me why everything here is as round as a ball?"

"Hush," said the man. "Don't speak so loudly. That's forbidden. Corners are forbidden, too, because the mayor is afraid he will bump into them. Therefore, everything must be rounded off."

"My goodness," whispered Sillibill, "in this city everything seems to be forbidden. What's going on here?"

"Whatever our mayor doesn't like he forbids. Whoever breaks the rules is locked up for three days in the cage which you see up there on the Town Hall tower."

"That beats everything," cried Sillibill. "Why do you put up with it?"

"Ssh," said the man, putting his finger to his lips, "questions are also forbidden." He then ran quickly down the street.

By then it was evening, and no one was to be seen in the streets. The full moon was shining. Its light fell on yet another sign. It said: DON'T MAKE MUSIC.

"Too much is too much!" cried Sillibill. He took out one of his crayons and drew a thick line through the DON'T so that it now read: MAKE MUSIC. "What a wonderful idea," thought Sillibill, and he began to cross out all the DON'T's on all the signs in the city.

By morning, everything forbidden was
now allowed. Signs that before had said:
DON'T ASK QUESTIONS, now said:
ASK QUESTIONS. Signs that had said:
BALLGAMES NOT ALLOWED, now said:
BALLGAMES ALLOWED.

Then Sillibill ran up the Town Hall
steps and stood there playing a happy
dance tune on his fiddle. At these
strange sounds all the windows and
doors flew open, and young and old
ran to the Town Hall square. When the
people saw that everything forbidden
was now allowed, they jumped up and
down with joy.

> They sang.
> They played.
> They laughed.
> They danced.

And candy and cookies were sold
throughout the town.

Then they brought the mean mayor
out of the Town Hall and put him into
the cage high up on the tower.

That was all very nice—only, there
seemed to be no end to the celebrating.
Nobody ever thought of getting back
to work.

The baker didn't bake.

The butcher's meat went bad.

The shops were closed.

The dirt in the streets
    piled up since nobody
    cleaned them.

And a house burned down
    because the firefighters
    wouldn't stop dancing.

When Sillibill saw what was happening,
he was very upset. He stopped playing.
But the people kept shouting, "Play on,
play on! We want to dance!"

Sillibill saw that he had done something the wrong way again. People couldn't go on singing and dancing for ever and ever! Sadly he cried,

"OH, I WISH WE ALL HAD MORE COMMON SENSE!"

At that—all of a sudden—the whole crowd stood still as if they had just been surprised out of a dream. Quietly everyone went back to work, and in a little while the whole town was back in order.

But the town was not the same. It had changed from a sad town to a happy one. People sang while they worked. They were happy and of good cheer.

Sillibill stood on the steps of the Town Hall and laughed. "For once I seem to have done something smart. I made a good wish. Now I can go home to my mother."

But just then, three people came up to him and said, "You are the smartest person in town. Therefore, the people have picked you for their mayor." With these words, one of them put the mayor's golden chain around Sillibill's neck. The second one put the town's ring on Sillibill's finger, and the third one put the mayor's hat on Sillibill's head.

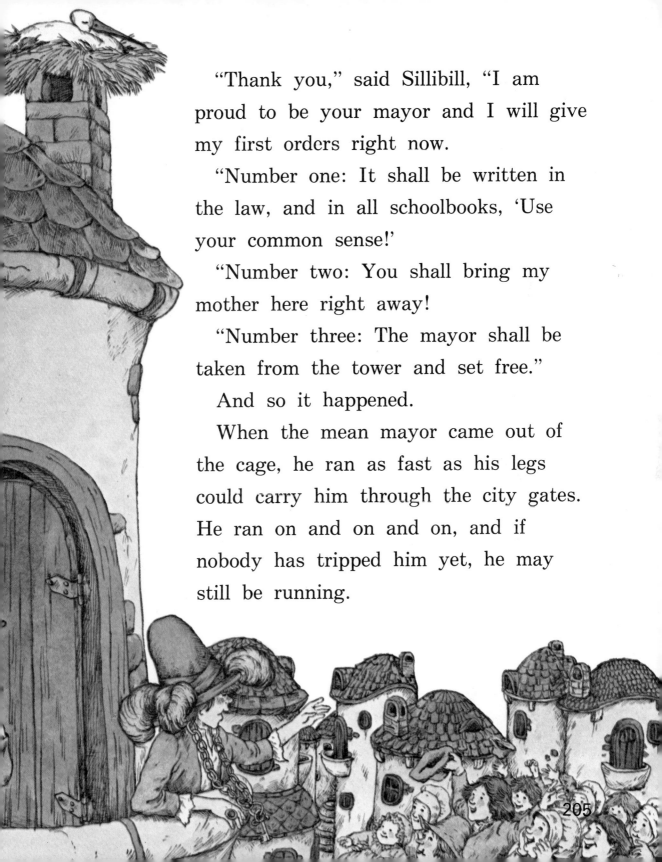

"Thank you," said Sillibill, "I am proud to be your mayor and I will give my first orders right now.

"Number one: It shall be written in the law, and in all schoolbooks, 'Use your common sense!'

"Number two: You shall bring my mother here right away!

"Number three: The mayor shall be taken from the tower and set free."

And so it happened.

When the mean mayor came out of the cage, he ran as fast as his legs could carry him through the city gates. He ran on and on and on, and if nobody has tripped him yet, he may still be running.

Adventures of ISABEL

Isabel met an enormous bear;
Isabel, Isabel, didn't care.
The bear was hungry, the bear was ravenous,
The bear's big mouth was cruel and cavernous.
The bear said, Isabel, glad to meet you,
How do, Isabel, now I'll eat you!
Isabel, Isabel, didn't worry,
Isabel didn't scream or scurry.
She washed her hands and she straightened
    her hair up,
Then Isabel quietly ate the bear up.

—Ogden Nash

THE CASE OF THE WHISTLING GHOST

Donald J. Sobol

Fabius Ray crawled slowly into Encyclopedia Brown's Detective Agency.

Encyclopedia, son of Idaville's top detective, was in no way surprised to see Fabius so close to the ground. During the summer, Fabius almost always went about on his hands and knees.

Fabius looked for bugs of all kinds. Nobody in Idaville knew more about the hidden feelings of bugs than Fabius.

Encyclopedia watched Fabius staring at the bug until he couldn't stand it any longer.

"What is it?" Encyclopedia cried.

"Ssh," whispered Fabius, crawling closer to the bug.

"Well, what is it?"

"Just a stinkbug," whispered Fabius. "Ooops! You scared him off!"

"Sorry about that," said Encyclopedia.

Fabius stood up sadly. But upon looking around and seeing where he was, he cheered up at once.

"Encyclopedia! Boy, I'm glad that bug led me here." He put down twenty-five cents. "I've been meaning to hire you."

"No case is too small," said Encyclopedia, hoping Fabius didn't take him at his word. Fabius might want a horsefly sent to jail. "What's the problem?"

"Somebody stole my camera," said Fabius. "And I think it was a ghost."

Encyclopedia stared at Fabius. "A g-ghost? *Where?*"

"In the old, deserted Potter house," said Fabius.

Encyclopedia laughed. "I don't believe in ghosts. I believe in facts."

"The facts," said Fabius. "Yesterday I went into the old house to hunt for bugs. I was about to take a picture of a spider when this ghost came down the stairs."

"You got the shakes and ran out of the house, leaving the camera behind?" said Encyclopedia.

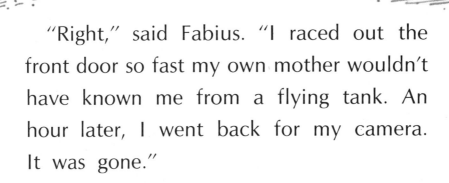

"Right," said Fabius. "I raced out the front door so fast my own mother wouldn't have known me from a flying tank. An hour later, I went back for my camera. It was gone."

"Did you notice anything special about the ghost?"

"It was white as a sheet," said Fabius. "And it was making scary noises and whistling at the same time."

"The ghost might have been a dog trainer when he was alive," said Encyclopedia. "Let's go to the old Potter house and look around."

The two boys left the agency. Fabius got his bike, and the two boys rode to the "haunted" house. On the way they passed the home of Rocky Smith, one of the Tigers, the meanest gang in town.

After two more blocks they came to
the old Potter place. The big house had
not been lived in for sixty years. It was
an old wooden building looking for a place
to fall down.

The boys rested their bikes against a pine tree. They walked through the high grass and weeds, up onto the old front porch, and into the dark front hall.

"I left my camera at the foot of the stairs while I explored," said Fabius. "When I came back for it, there was the ghost, whistling and making strange noises."

He led the way into the kitchen.

"I wanted to photograph that!" he said, pointing to the back door.

Encyclopedia gasped. Across the bottom half of the door a spider had spun a beautiful, wheel-shaped web.

"The best work I have ever seen by a ray spider," said Fabius in a glow.

While Fabius looked at the spider web, Encyclopedia returned to the front hall. He found footprints in the heavy dust on the stairs.

"Ghosts don't wear shoes," he thought out loud. "At least not in the summer."

"How's that?" called Fabius. "Did you find a clue?"

"Your ghost left footprints," said Encyclopedia, as Fabius hurried from the kitchen. "I think I know who it was."

"You're smarter than the FBI!" cried Fabius. "Who was it?"

"A boy who saw you come here with your camera yesterday," said Encyclopedia. "Rocky Smith."

"Aw, a lot of people could have seen me go into the house yesterday," said Fabius. "Why Rocky Smith?"

"Because he lives close to this old house; because he's a member of the Tigers; and because he knocked out two front teeth a few days ago trying to break into a parked car."

"I heard that his screwdriver slipped and hit him in the mouth," said Fabius. "But what have two missing front teeth got to do with it?"

"Without his two front teeth," explained Encyclopedia, "whenever Rocky says the letter *S,* he *whistles.*"

"The ape!" yelled Fabius, hopping angrily up and down. "That rat in a bed-sheet!"

"Take it easy," said Encyclopedia. "We haven't any proof—yet. I want to hear what Rocky has to say for himself."

When the two boys got to the Smith house, Rocky was sitting on the ground gasping. He had just tried to kick a cat and missed, twisting his foot.

"You dressed up in a sheet and scared me in the old Potter house yesterday," said Fabius.

"Then you stole his camera," said Encyclopedia. "I'll bet a lot of people saw you go up the front porch. So don't say you didn't!"

Rocky's face showed how hard he was struggling for something to say.

"Sure," he said, whistling a little. "Sure I saw you go inside. Another kid, carrying a sheet, went in just behind you. Pretty soon you sailed out. I went inside to find out what was the matter. In the front hall I saw this other kid pick up a camera. When he saw me, he ran out the back door and into the woods."

"That's a good story," said Encyclopedia. "Good enough to prove you were the one that stole the camera!"

(To find out how Encyclopedia knew that Rocky was the ghost, turn to the Contents of this book. Then find the title "Answers" and its page number.)

HIT and RUN

Kate and Jim walked to the park,
And on the corner they met Clark.
Clark then walked with Kate and Jim,
And soon they stopped to take a swim.

While at the pool, they all asked Mark
To go with them down to the park,
Mark said, sure, he'd love to go,
He'd even bring his best friend Joe.

They all then went to buy some candy,
And Kate saw Mary, Sue, and Andy,
Who said they'd like to play some ball
If they could please bring Gail and Paul.

218

Each one agreed, and off they went,
And soon they met their good friend Kent.
But Kent said no, he couldn't go
For he was going to a show.

Soon they all got to the park,
But it was getting very dark,
And Clark and Jim and Sue and Joe
Decided it was time to go.

So they went home, and all the rest
Talked it over and thought it best
To choose two teams and play some ball
Until they couldn't see at all.

Soon it was time to start the game,
But first the teams each chose a name.
One was "HIT," the other "RUN"———
Now—how many were on each one?

—Dina Anastasio

(For the answer, look up "Answers" in the Contents of this book.)

SILENT VISITOR

Theodore Brauner

This is a true story. It happened to a photographer while he was working in the Middle East.

Part One
ADVENTURE

FIRST NIGHT

Nothing told me that something strange was about to begin that first morning. I just walked into my kitchen and there it was. The bananas in my fruit basket were gone, or at least all but the skins were gone. And I had not eaten them.

First I thought of the children who lived in the building and played in the garden below. I often talked with them when I met them in the

halls and on the stairs. Could they be playing a trick on me? Maybe. And yet, there was no way they could have reached my kitchen without my knowing it. The kitchen window was too high, and I knew that they had not come in the door.

I puzzled and puzzled. I lived alone and had no pets. None of my friends had been in to see me. There were no mice in the building; at least none I knew of.

Still, the bananas were gone. And why bananas and nothing else?

Who or what had been in my apartment? I could not guess.

SECOND NIGHT

Could it happen again? I wondered. And suddenly I knew that I could learn what had happened only if it happened again.

Hoping that it would, I laid my plans carefully. That night I placed the fruit in the basket, just as they had been the night before. There were oranges, bananas, and other fruit.

I also left some meat, cheese, bread, and sugar on the plate. I left a little bowl of milk, too. Then I closed the kitchen door and began the wait till morning.

The long night passed slowly, but at last it was gone. I hurried to the kitchen. What I saw excited me. My visitor had come again, and again only the bananas had been eaten.

I looked quickly around for a clue as to who my caller might have been. But all I saw was the kitchen window, open as always. It was an owl, I thought. It could have been an owl. An owl could have come in through the window.

Then I looked at the skins and changed my mind. There were holes in the skins; not holes made by a beak, but holes made by teeth.

THIRD NIGHT

How could I find out what it was? A camera! That was it. I could take a picture. Or rather, since I could not be there, the creature could photograph itself.

I went to work at once. I set up the camera and pointed it at the fruit basket. I placed the flashgun in a place where it would light the

fruit. And then I tried to decide how to make the flashbulb burn at the right time.

I put some new bananas in the basket and set one edge of the basket on a small ball. I ran wires from the flash to the basket. Now, when my visitor touched the bananas, the camera would take its picture.

When night came, I closed the door to the kitchen, and sat down in the living room. It would be another long wait.

The time passed slowly. At last I felt I could go to see what had happened. I walked quickly into the kitchen, and looked at the flashbulb. It was burned.

When I saw the picture I was very surprised. The creature was something I had never thought of at all. It was a bat.

FOURTH NIGHT

I decided not to trap the bat, and not to drive it off. Instead, I would try to take more photographs. What I really wanted was a picture of my visitor while it ate.

Again I set up the camera and waited out the evening.

The next morning the photograph showed just what I had hoped it would. The animal was eating a banana. But to my surprise the creature did not look like a bat; it looked more like a squirrel.

I had always heard that bats were blind; but this animal had a well-formed open eye. Bats have wings, although I had been told that they did not fly as high as my fifth floor apartment. The wings on this creature were not clear, although they might have been there. On the other hand, a squirrel would have no wings at all and could not have gotten to my window in any way.

I didn't know what to think.

225

FIFTH NIGHT

Another picture was the only answer. I set
up my camera once again on the fifth night.
Once again, the flashbulb burned.

The picture I saw the next morning proved,
once and for all, that my visitor really was
a bat. The creature was different from any
ideas I had had of bats, however.

It was a friendly-looking creature. Its head
looked soft and pleasant, its eyes large and
kind. It might have been a squirrel or a deer.
Only the wings made it a bat.

That day I showed my pictures to a
scientist. He knew at once what it was: a
fruit bat.

There are many kinds of bats. Mine belonged
to a group that eats only fruit. They see quite
well in the daytime, but do not see so well
at night. At night they find their way by giving
out clicking sounds that echo back to them
from walls and things in the air.

The fruit bat lives about twelve years. The
mother bat will have a baby once a year. Most
of them live in the Middle East.

SIXTH NIGHT

I had become quite fond of the bat, by now. I had even given it a name: *Russet*. I did not want to keep Russet as a pet. I did not even want it in my kitchen every night forever. But I did want to learn as much as I could about it.

The picture taken this night gave me a clearer idea of Russet's wings. It told me more, but not enough.

SEVENTH NIGHT

On the seventh night, I went to the kitchen to see if a picture had been taken. As I stepped in the door, something moved in the corner, and I pointed my flashlight toward it. It was Russet, clinging to the wall. My chance had come.

I stepped closer to the corner. Russet did not move. I went closer again, and then again. Still Russet stayed. I reached out. The fur on Russet's back was soft. The body fur was light gray-brown; the wings, dark gray.

Its wings opened to about a foot. Its body was about four and a half inches long.

My hand closed gently over the small body. I picked it up and brought it toward me to look at it more closely. It shivered with fear. So I put it down upon the fruit. But it did not stay. It flew up and out the window.

EIGHTH AND NINTH NIGHTS

Russet stayed away.

TENTH NIGHT

The pictures from the tenth night showed a strange shape against Russet's body. What could it be?

ELEVENTH NIGHT

I wanted to take a good picture of the
strange shape I had seen. Two pictures taken
at the same time would be the only answer.
Two cameras were set up. Both would take
a picture when the flashbulb burned.

Just as I had hoped, my plan worked. Two
pictures were taken, and in both I saw the
small shape clearly. I thought I knew what the
small shape was. But I wanted to be sure.

That afternoon I took the pictures to the
scientist. He looked at them and told me I
was right. The small shape was indeed a
baby bat.

I wanted, of course, to get more pictures
of both Russet and her baby. But after the
eleventh night, they never came again.

Part Two
DISCOVERY

I waited for many days and looked each night
for Russet. But she did not appear. Where had
she come from, and why did she now stay away?
The question of where she had come from was
the one I thought about most. Where might bats
live in the city? There were no barns and no
caves for them to hide in. My friends were as
curious as I, and we all began to look for
places where bats might be.

After searching for a long time, three of my
friends found places where bats of some kind
were known to live. Through all the nights
that Russet had been coming, I had been
studying the visits carefully. I knew just when
she came. What was more important was that I
knew she came twice each night. I knew how fast
Russet could fly, and also knew that there had
been about half an hour between the two visits
she had paid me each night. If she had gone
home during this time, only one of the three
places seemed near enough.

As soon as I had worked this out, Joe, the one who had found the place, and I went to see what it was like.

The place where the bats lived was an old, empty well, with a ladder going down into it. We walked around and felt the ladder. It seemed strong enough, but even if it had not, we would not have given up. We started down together, Joe following me.

We went down and down and down. The air grew dank, full of a strong animal smell. The ladder was not so strong as we had thought. It shook at each step, and we had to move with care. But we went on.

Ten feet from the bottom, eighty feet down, we came to a group of bats. There were hundreds of them, crowded around a small hole in the wall of the well. This hole, we could see, led to a tunnel, a tunnel that for some reason had been walled in and could now be reached only by the small hole that had worn through. The bats rested in large numbers around the hole, inside the well, and in even larger numbers, as far as we could tell, in the tunnel.

There were bats all around us. And all of them hung upside-down. We had come to the right place.

The light around was dim, but bright enough for us to see the bats quite clearly.

Some of the bats scratched themselves, grabbing bits of fur in their teeth. Others were in twos, tightly hugging each other. One group moved their heads back and forth and seemed to whisper secrets to each other. Others played different kinds of games with each other.

At the beginning I was quiet. I did not want to frighten the creatures before I got pictures of them. But finally I needed pictures with more life. To frighten them into flying, I shouted. Nothing happened. We banged our feet against the ladder, and it shook more than the bats did. We waved our handkerchiefs. But nothing made the bats move.

I took a few more pictures, hanging as far from the ladder and as close to the bats as I could get. Then we called it a day. I had seen the place, I was sure, that Russet had come from. As for Russet herself, I could not be sure. Maybe she was in the tunnel. Maybe she was one of those I had seen. I did not know, and I felt fairly sure that I would probably never know.

We began to climb slowly up, Joe and I. But a short way up I stopped. For there on the wall before me, apart from the other bats, was a bat alone. It lay flat against the wall, head up, wings spread and still. Could this be Russet? My scientist friend had said that

mothers often stayed apart from the rest of the
bats. And this one was surely apart. It seemed
almost not to belong with the other bats at all.

I looked at the bat for some time and it did
not move. I reached out and patted its back.
Still it did not move. Almost sure now that
it was Russet, I picked up one wing and then
I saw the baby.

Still Russet did not move; she looked at me
and then, without hurry, left the wall. She
flew once around the well, then rose up into
the night. I watched until she became one with
the other bats rising into the night air.

Part Three

A FEW WORDS ABOUT BATS

It was long believed, and still is in many places, that all bats are blind. "Blind as a bat" is often heard. Long ago, scientists watching bats and seeing how well they found their way around could not explain how bats "saw."

Later, studies showed that some bats, at least, could see very well. But it was then shown that even these bats when blindfolded

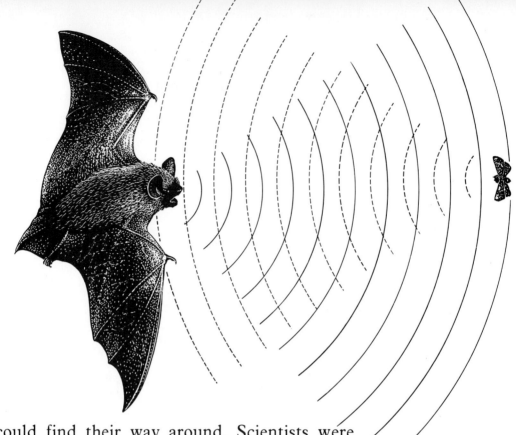

could find their way around. Scientists were
more puzzled than ever and said as a joke:
"Bats can see with their ears."

This was not as funny as it seemed. Most
bats make a sound that is too high for our
ears to hear. They screech as they move
around, and the echoes of these cries come back
to their ears. In this way they are able to tell
where walls and other things are.

Bats can almost always find their way home.
The caves or trees in which they live often
have small holes into which the bats fly.

Sometimes the hole is less than a foot across, and, in the case of a cave, may be hidden by bushes and trees. Yet bats flying at night can find their way to such a hole from as much as one hundred and fifty miles away. How they do this, no one knows.

Bats go out to feed at night. In the daytime they hang close together in their caves, trees, or other dark places where they make their homes. Only when evening comes do they begin to stir. First a few will rise up and fly around, sometimes going out of the hole into the night above. Then others will begin to move. And finally all of the bats will rise up in a body and fly high into the air. There they go their own ways to spend the night searching for whatever food they like best. In the morning they come home from their night of work to sleep until the next night.

Which Word Would You Use?

Some words sound the same. But they have different meanings. They have different spellings, too. You have to read the whole sentence to know how to say the word and what it means.

> I liked the clown at the circus.
> The bird watched me with one eye.

The words *I* and *eye* sound alike. But they have different meanings and different spellings.

Read each word in the box. Then read each sentence. Choose the word that makes the sentence correct. Write the whole sentence on your paper.

> blew   blue

1. The sky was very ____ all day.
   1. The sky was very blue all day.
2. The wind ____ the leaves on the tree.
3. Isabel wore a ____ dress to school.

sun	son

4. Abe gave his ____ a green balloon.

5. Plants need light from the ____ to grow.

sea	see

6. The ____ was too rough for the sailboat.

7. Did you ____ Carmen when she came in?

right	write

8. Tom has to ____ a letter to Aunt Alice.

9. Allen used the ____ word in the puzzle.

whole	hole

10. John cut a ____ in the box for a door.

11. The ____ class took a trip to the zoo.

eight	ate

12. I ____ everything on my plate.

13. There were ____ people at the party.

CHARLES RIVER

BEACON STREET

MT. VERNON STREET

LOUISBURG SQUARE

CORNER BOOKSHOP

BEACON HILL

STATE HOUSE

PUBLIC GARDEN

CHARLES STREET

BOSTON COMMON

MAKE WAY FOR DUCKLINGS

Robert McCloskey

Make Way for Ducklings *is a very famous story. It was written about forty years ago. Since it was written, many, many children have read and enjoyed the story.*

The story was based on something that really happened. It didn't happen in exactly the same way that it does in the story. But ducklings did once walk through the streets of Boston.

On the opposite page, you will see a map of Boston. It shows the places that are talked about in the story. When you have read Make Way for Ducklings, *look at the map again. See if you can find where the ducklings walked.*

Part One

A Place to Live

Mr. and Mrs. Mallard were looking for a place to live. But every time Mr. Mallard saw what looked like a nice place, Mrs. Mallard said it was no good. There were sure to be foxes in the woods or turtles in the water. And she was not going to raise a family where there might be foxes or turtles. So they flew on and on.

When they got to Boston, they felt too tired to fly any further. There was a nice pond in the Public Garden, with a little island on it. "The very place to spend the night," quacked Mr. Mallard. So down they flapped.

Next morning they fished for their breakfast
in the mud at the bottom of the pond. But
they didn't find much.

Just as they were getting ready to start on
their way, a strange enormous bird came by.
It was pushing a boat full of people. And there
was a man sitting on its back. "Good
morning," quacked Mr. Mallard, being polite.
The big bird was too proud to answer. But the

people on the boat threw peanuts into the water. So the Mallards followed them all round the pond and got another breakfast, better than the first.

"I like this place," said Mrs. Mallard as they climbed out on the bank and waddled along. "Why don't we build a nest and raise our ducklings right in this pond? There are no foxes and no turtles, and the people feed us peanuts. What could be better?"

"Good," said Mr. Mallard, delighted that at last Mrs. Mallard had found a place that suited her. But—

"Look out!" squawked Mrs. Mallard, all of a dither. "You'll get run over!" And when she got her breath she added: "*This* is no place for babies, with all those horrid things rushing about. We'll have to look somewhere else!"

So they flew over Beacon Hill and round the State House. But there was no place there.

They looked in Louisburg Square. But there was no water to swim in.

Then they flew over the Charles River. "This is better," quacked Mr. Mallard. "That island looks like a nice quiet place, and it's only a little way from the Public Garden."

"Yes," said Mrs. Mallard, remembering the peanuts. "That looks like just the right place to hatch ducklings."

So they chose a cozy spot among the bushes near the water and settled down to build their nest. And only just in time, for now they were

beginning to molt. All their old wing feathers started to drop out. They would not be able to fly again until the new ones grew in.

But of course they could swim, and one day they swam over to the park on the river bank. And there they met a policeman called Michael. Michael fed them peanuts, and after that the Mallards called on Michael every day.

After Mrs. Mallard had laid eight eggs in the nest, she couldn't go to visit Michael any more, because she had to sit on the eggs to keep them warm. She moved off the nest only to get a drink of water, or to have her lunch, or to count the eggs and make sure they were all there.

One day the ducklings hatched out. First came Jack, then Kack, and then Lack, then Mack and Nack and Ouack and Pack and Quack. Mr. and Mrs. Mallard were bursting with pride. It was a great responsibility taking care of so many ducklings. It kept them very busy.

Part Two
Michael Helps Out

One day Mr. Mallard decided he'd like to take a trip to see what the rest of the river was like, further down. So off he set. "I'll meet you in a week, in the Public Garden," he quacked over his shoulder. "Take good care of the ducklings."

"Don't you worry," said Mrs. Mallard. "I know all about bringing up children." And she did.

She taught them how to swim and dive.

She taught them to walk in a line, to come when they were called, and to keep a safe distance from bikes and scooters and other things with wheels.

When at last she felt perfectly satisfied with them, she said one morning: "Come along, children. Follow me."

Before you could wink an eyelash, Jack, Kack, Lack, Mack, Nack, Ouack, Pack, and Quack fell into line, just as they had been taught. Mrs. Mallard led the way into the water. And they swam behind her to the opposite bank.

There they waded ashore and waddled along till they came to the highway.

Mrs. Mallard stepped out to cross the road. "Honk, honk!" went the horns on the speeding cars. "Qua-a-ack!" went Mrs. Mallard as she tumbled back again.

"Quack! Quack! Quack! Quack!" went Jack,
Kack, Lack, Mack, Nack, Ouack, Pack, and
Quack, just as loud as their little quackers
could quack. The cars kept speeding by and
honking. And Mrs. Mallard and the ducklings
kept right on quack-quack-quacking.

They made such a noise that Michael came
running, waving his arms and blowing his
whistle.

He planted himself in the center of the
road, raised one hand to stop the traffic, and
then beckoned with the other, the way
policemen do, for Mrs. Mallard to cross over.

As soon as Mrs. Mallard and the ducklings were safe on the other side and on their way down Mount Vernon Street, Michael rushed back to his police booth.

He called Clancy at headquarters and said: "There's a family of ducks walkin' down the street!"

Clancy said: "Family of *what*?"

"*Ducks*!" yelled Michael. "Send a police car, quick!"

Meanwhile, Mrs. Mallard had reached the Corner Book Shop and turned into Charles Street, with Jack, Kack, Lack, Mack, Nack, Ouack, Pack, and Quack all marching in line behind her.

Everyone stared. An old lady from Beacon Hill said: "Isn't it amazing!" And the man who swept the streets said: "Well, now, ain't that nice!" And when Mrs. Mallard heard them she was so proud she tipped her nose in the air and walked along with an extra swing in her waddle.

When they came to the corner of Beacon Street, there was the police car with four policemen that Clancy had sent from headquarters. The policemen held back the traffic so Mrs. Mallard and the ducklings could march across the street, right on into the Public Garden.

Inside the gate they all turned round to say thank you to the policemen. The policemen smiled and waved good-by.

When they reached the pond and swam across to the little island, there was Mr. Mallard waiting for them, just as he had promised.

The ducklings liked the new island so much that they decided to live there. All day long they follow the swan boats and eat peanuts. And when night falls, they swim to their little island and go to sleep.

Debbie, Ann, and Norman

As you read a story carefully, you are able to understand more than just the words. You are able to tell how one person is different from another person. You are also able to tell how they are alike. Read these stories.

Debbie and Ann are sisters. They both have brown hair and eyes. Debbie walks to a school near her house. But Ann takes a bus to a special art school. Ann paints lovely pictures. Someday, Ann would like to be a famous artist like Mary Cassatt.

Norman lives next door to Debbie and Ann. Debbie and Norman are in the same class at school. On Saturday mornings, Norman goes to dancing class. He is a very good dancer. He does old and new dances. On Saturday afternoons, Norman and Debbie play football. Norman is the best player on the team. But someday, Norman would like to be a famous dancer like Fred Astaire.

Read each question. Choose the correct answer.
Write the answer on your paper.

1. How is Ann different from Debbie?
   Ann plays football with Norman.
   Ann has brown hair and brown eyes.
   Ann has a special ability to paint.

2. How is Norman different from Ann and Debbie?
   Norman plays football on Saturday.
   Norman goes to a dancing class.
   Norman goes to a special art school.

3. How are Debbie and Ann alike?
   They both walk to school.
   They both go to a special art school.
   They both live next door to Norman.

4. How are Norman and Debbie alike?
   They both go to dancing classes.
   They both play football on Saturday.
   They both paint lovely pictures.

5. How are Ann and Norman alike?
   Both want to be like famous people.
   Both want to paint famous pictures.
   Both want to be famous football players.

WHAT DOES A TWO-HUNDRED-POUND MOUSE SAY?

Use puppets to make plays from these jokes. Make your puppet move, clap, boo, or anything else you can think of to make the plays funny. What Puppet 1 *says is always printed in capital and lowercase letters. What* Puppet 2 *says is always printed in capital letters.*

1. **Puppet 1** to **Puppet 2:**
   I know a man who had snew in his blood.
   Puppet 2: WHAT'S SNEW?
   Puppet 1: Nothing. What's new with you?

2. Do you know what Tommy was doing this morning?
   NO, WHAT?
   He was standing in front of the mirror with his eyes closed so he could see what he looks like when he's asleep.

3. I bet I can make you say "black."
I BET YOU CAN'T.
What's the color of the American flag?
RED, WHITE, AND BLUE.
See, I told you I could make you say "blue."
NO, YOU SAID I'D SAY "BLACK."
You just did.

4. Pete and Repeat went for a boat ride. Pete fell in. Who was left?
REPEAT.
Pete and Repeat went for a boat ride. Pete fell in. Who was left?
REPEAT.
Pete and Repeat . . .

5. Sammy?
YES, TEACHER.
If you found a quarter in one pocket, and forty cents in the other, what would you have?
SOMEBODY ELSE'S PANTS.

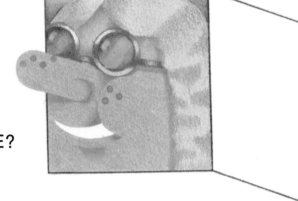

6. Knock, knock.
   WHO'S THERE?
   Red.
   RED WHO?
   Red pepper. Isn't that a hot one?

7. Say, Daddy owl,
   I'm worried about
   baby owl.
   WHY IS THAT,
   MOMMY OWL?
   He doesn't give a hoot about anything.

8. What does a duck do when it flies
   upside down?
   IT QUACKS UP.

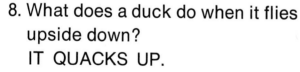

266

9. Watch out! There's a henweigh
on your neck!
WHAT'S A HENWEIGH?
About three pounds.

10. What does a two-hundred-pound mouse say?
HERE, KITTY, KITTY.

11. Ask me if I'm a boat.
    ARE YOU A BOAT?
    Yes, now ask me if I'm an
    airplane.
    ARE YOU AN AIRPLANE?
    No, I just told you I'm a boat!

12. There were two skunks——
    When In was out,
    Out was in.
    One day Out was in
    and In was out.
    Their mother,
    who was in with Out,
    wanted In in.
    "Bring In in,"
    she said to Out.
    So Out went out
    and brought In in.
    "How did you find him so
    fast?" she asked.
    "Instinct," he said.

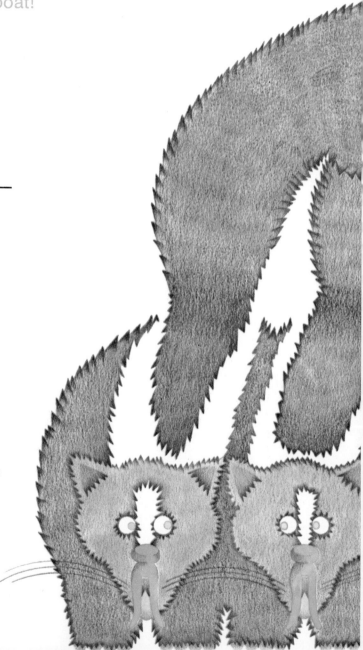

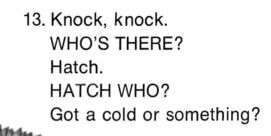

13. Knock, knock.
WHO'S THERE?
Hatch.
HATCH WHO?
Got a cold or something?

14. I keep seeing spots before my eyes.
HAVE YOU SEEN A DOCTOR?
No, just spots.

These are just a few of the things that you can use in your puppet show. Add your own riddles, jokes, knock-knocks, or stories. Remember that the show should move quickly. Do not wait too long between jokes. A good way to end your show is to have all the puppets sing a silly song.

ALASKA

The Land of Many Riches

Y. Kim Choi

In 1869, the American Secretary of State, William Seward, did something that many people thought was foolish. He bought a huge piece of land called Alaska. He bought Alaska from Russia for only two cents an acre. But many people thought it was a waste of money. To them, Alaska was just a useless land of rocks, snow, and ice. They even called it "Seward's Folly."

271

However, the following years have proved these people wrong. Alaska has been worth much more than it cost because of the many riches that have been discovered there.

Some of the greatest riches are the trees in Alaska's forests. One third of Alaskan land is covered by forests. The trees are cut and sold to all parts of the world.

The sea around Alaska is full of riches, too. Many fish and sea animals live there. Each year, large numbers of codfish, herring, halibut, crabs, and shrimp are caught. They are sold to the rest of the United States and to the world.

Other riches are found underground. Gold was discovered about one hundred years ago, and many people first came to Alaska in search of gold. Even though gold is still mined, other minerals, such as iron, coal, silver, copper, and tin, are now more important. But the oil and natural gas discovered in 1968 are the most important of all the underground riches.

Alaska is by far the largest state of the United States. It's as large as Texas, California, and Montana put together. Much of Alaska is covered by mountains. Many of them are snowcapped throughout the year. Many glaciers sparkle along the valleys and sides of these mountains. Over a long period of time, these glaciers have moved slowly down to the coast and have cut many deep bays.

The name *Alaska* comes from a native word that means "the great land." It is a fitting name for the state. Alaska is truly great, not only in its size, but also in its riches. Today, most Americans would agree that Alaska was one of the biggest bargains in American history.

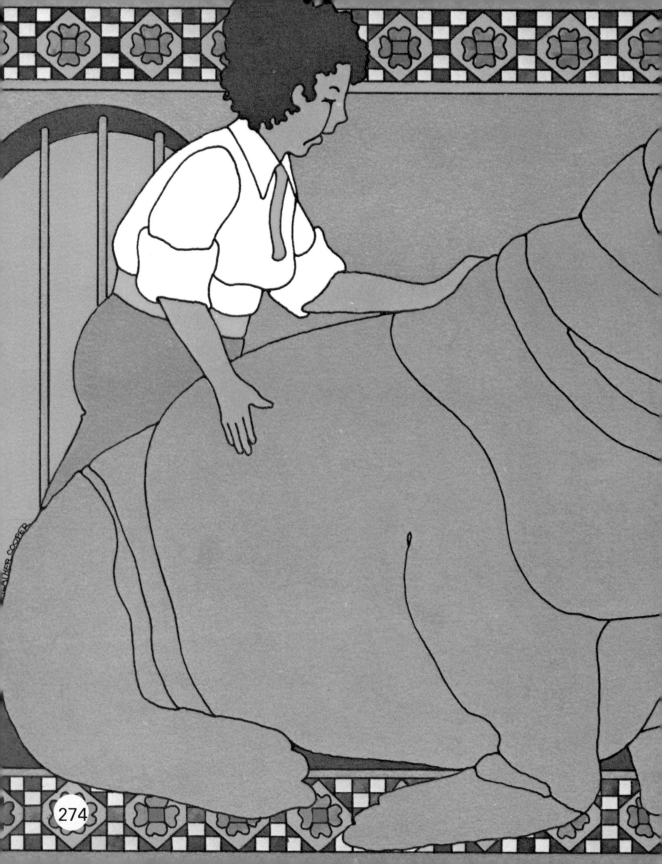

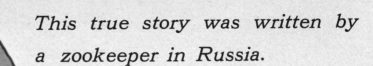

This true story was written by a zookeeper in Russia.

 # Nyurka The Walrus

Vera Chaplina

Nyurka was funny and fat like all walruses. Her round wet eyes gave her a very funny look. She appeared stupid but she was really very smart.

She had made a long trip to the zoo by boat and train, locked in a small wooden crate without any water. She arrived tired, and had large, open sores on her back and sides.

I washed her sores. I fed her cleaned fish that were cut into small pieces, which she took from my hands bit by bit. What noises she made! They sounded like corks popping from a bottle.

Nyurka ate from nine to ten pounds of fish every day, sometimes even more. Maybe because I fed her, Nyurka soon got used to me and knew me from far away. She would greet me with deep, sharp hoots, something like a dog's bark, and would hurry to meet me, waddling around on her flippers.

She was quick to learn, quicker even than some dogs. Nyurka did not like being left alone in her cage. And when I started to leave after feeding her, she would cover the door with her body and cry out loudly.

I had to trick her. I would bring in the food and place it in the far corner of her cage. Then, as soon as Nyurka started to eat, I would run out quickly. But the trick did not work for long because she very soon caught onto it. After only a few days she worked out the problem by jumping into the water. And since she could swim across the pool faster than I could go around it, she was at the door before me, pressing her body against it, trying not to let me leave. Have you ever tried to push aside a 325-pound walrus?

Nyurka kept me in the cage until she tired of playing. First she would ask me to go for a swim. Then she would try to push me in with her nose. She didn't want to go alone into the small and rather lonely pool.

Most of her day was spent sleeping at the edge of the pool. In order to make her move about more, I decided to take her for walks. But this wasn't as easy as it sounds. At first Nyurka wouldn't leave her cage. I opened the door, went out and called to her. She cried out as she looked at me, but she couldn't decide to come out the door. Using bits of fish as bait as I moved to the door, I finally got her out.

Our walks were short, since the sand bothered her flippers. But even so, she loved them. We would take our walk in the evening, after the whistle of the guards had closed the zoo. As soon as Nyurka heard the whistle she would start looking for me. Then she would run to meet me and help open the cage door. As I removed the lock, Nyurka would push the door open with her nose. She even learned to open the latch.

I didn't want to be bothered by her when it was time to clean up her cage. So I would push her out. Then I would lock myself in. At first, she cried. Later, in trying to get back in, she found that she could push the latch with a strong whack of her nose and open the door herself.

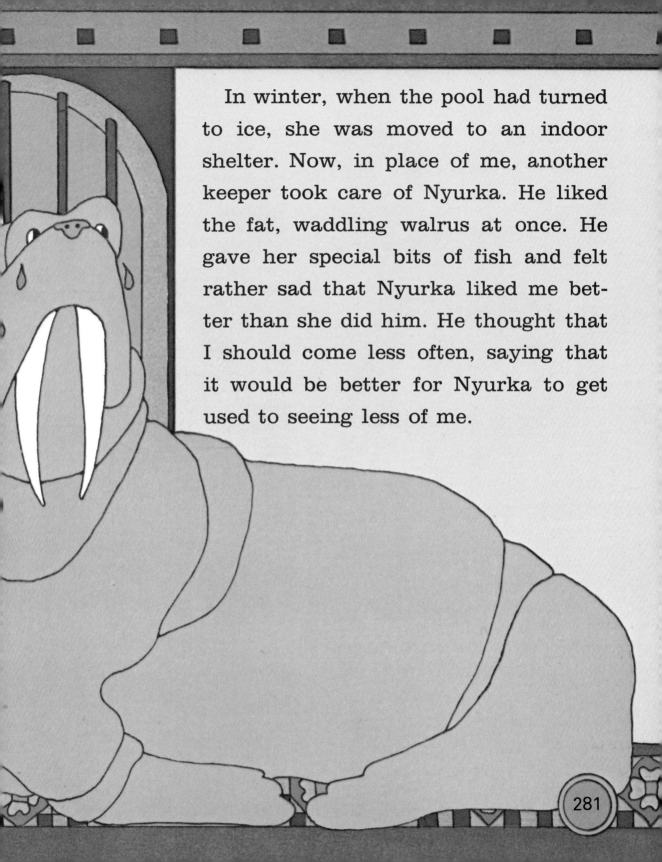

In winter, when the pool had turned to ice, she was moved to an indoor shelter. Now, in place of me, another keeper took care of Nyurka. He liked the fat, waddling walrus at once. He gave her special bits of fish and felt rather sad that Nyurka liked me better than she did him. He thought that I should come less often, saying that it would be better for Nyurka to get used to seeing less of me.

Rather than hurt the other keeper's feelings, I did stay away. Nyurka needed time to get used to him, too. Weeks went by. I was lonely for my flippered friend, and I wondered if she would remember me.

One day as I was passing by, I decided to look in on Nyurka. She was lying in the water out of sight. From time to time the tip of her nose would appear above the water.

Very softly I called out, "Nyurka." Even though she was under water, she knew my voice at once and was out of the pool in a flash. She rose up, and before I could step out of the way, two flippers bore down heavily on my shoulders. Streams of water flowed over my coat as a fat, wet head pushed happily at my face. It was hard to catch my breath and even harder to keep from falling over.

When I had to leave, Nyurka ran to the screen, crying miserably. Later I was told that tears ran down her face and that she ate nothing for the rest of the day.

That evening Nyurka broke through the screen and got out into the hall. She opened one door, then another, went up the stairway and climbed out through the window to the roof. Her loud cries rang out in the stillness of the night. The guard called some people to help. They gently carried Nyurka downstairs and put her back in her cage.

The Sound of Night

Small is the sound of night,
And far away
From all the lively noisings
Of the day—
Lullaby,
Airplanes, whispering
In the sky,
Tip-toe footsteps,
Car on road,
The tiny hopscotch
Of a toad,
And in the winter
Time of year
Comes a silence
You can hear,
As the snow
Sifts on for hours,
Filling hollows,
Frilling towers,
Muffling footsteps,
Feathering air
Until there's stillness
Everywhere—
Then the hush becomes
The sound
Of snowflakes touching
On the ground...

—Mary O'Neill

THE ULTIMATE AUTO

Patrick McGivern

Part One
The Arrival

The mayor of the city of New York was writing a letter one day. All of a sudden a funny look came over her face.

"What's the matter?" said the mayor's secretary.

"I just had the feeling," the mayor said, shaking, "I just had the feeling that the Ultimate Auto has arrived in my city. The *Ultimate Auto*—you know what *that* means."

"I don't know what you're talking about," said the secretary.

"Well, look outside then," the mayor said, leading him to a window. "What do you see?"

"Just a lot of parked cars."

"Those cars aren't parked. That's moving traffic."

"But it isn't moving."

"*Almost* isn't moving. Look closely, you'll see those cars are crawling—maybe one foot a minute. That's moving. That's what traffic in this city is like every day. But when the Ultimate Auto gets to town—and we've been waiting for it for years—it will be just one car too many. The Ultimate Auto will jam in that traffic like a key in a lock, and every moving thing in the city will come to a stop. That will be the beginning of the biggest traffic jam in the world. I have nightmares about it. I even have daymares. And now I've got this crazy feeling that the Ultimate Auto is *here.*"

287

"But that's silly," said the secretary. "How can you really tell?"

"I can't, of course," the mayor said. "And you're right, it is silly—just one of those silly feelings you get sometimes. Well, what was I doing?"

"Writing a letter."

"Let's get back to that."

They did, and it would be hours before the mayor knew that her silly feeling was right.

Indeed, the Ultimate Auto had already arrived in New York. At that very second it was heading south on the highway at forty-seven miles an hour.

The Ultimate Auto was one of those little cars, painted gray. The driver was Samuel Smerb, forty-two years old, who worked for the Lincoln Animal Society in upstate New York.

Back at the dog pound, they were running low on Vitamin Z for the dogs' food, and Smerb was driving to New York City to pick up some more. Smerb did not like New York. It was too noisy, too smelly, and too crowded for his taste. And, above all, there was too much traffic on the streets.

To make the trip more fun, Smerb took eight of his four-footed friends along. The dogs were all finding the ride very pleasant, until Smerb turned the Ultimate Auto onto the West Side Highway.

"Hmmm," Smerb said. "The traffic is slowing down, and this is the *highway.* I wonder what it's like on the streets."

Smerb's friends said nothing, but he knew they were wondering, too.

Once they were off the West Side Highway, it took a whole hour to go three blocks along Forty-Second Street. Smerb could hardly see through the thick air.

He could hear nothing but screaming drivers, beeping police whistles, and the crazy blaring of car horns. A cat rested in the shade under Smerb's car. Someone leaned on the car, thinking it was parked there.

Then, turning down Fifth Avenue, Smerb headed the Ultimate Auto into a space between a big truck and a bus. It was just the right size for his small car, but the space kept getting smaller and smaller. Then the truck stopped. Then the bus stopped. Smerb stopped, too. So did the taxi behind him, and the Mother Mile's pie truck behind the taxi, and the police car behind the pie truck, and...well, everything came to a stop. In fact, not even a bicycyle could have moved on any street anywhere in the whole city.

An hour went by, and Smerb wished the taxi driver behind him would stop yelling and shaking his fist. Another hour went by, and Smerb tapped his fingers on the door window. Another hour went by, and Smerb finally blew his car horn. But he couldn't hear it over the noise of a thousand other horns.

It began to grow dark, and still nothing moved. Smerb decided to walk his four-footed friends. He turned off his little car, put on their leashes, and led them into the jammed street. Smerb saw a police officer and asked what was going on.

"It looks as if the Ultimate Auto has arrived in New York City," said Officer Madia.

"What's the Ultimate Auto?" asked Smerb.

"You'll find out tonight," said Madia, "when the mayor goes on television."

"I don't have a TV in the car," said Smerb.

"Forget about the car," said Madia. "You'd better find a place to stay for the night."

Smerb did—at the Hotel James. The room had a television set. At 8:30 P.M. the mayor appeared on every televison station in the city.

"My fellow New Yorkers," she began quietly, "the traffic problem in our city is...well, it's out of control." The mayor went on to explain what had happened and stated that everyone must be on the lookout for the Ultimate Auto.

"Tomorrow morning all the police officers in the city will be looking for the car, and helicopters and planes will join in from the air. I promise you that I will do everything in my power to get the traffic moving again. As a first step, no more tickets will be given for speeding. And you may be pleased to know, my fellow New Yorkers, that I have fired the secretary of traffic control."

Part Two
A Key in a Lock

The next morning, as planes and helicopters flew overhead, Smerb and his friends went back to their car. The taxi driver was still there, banging his horn and shaking his fist at Smerb's empty car. Officer Madia was there, too, and he looked miserable.

"They tell me that it may take weeks to find the Ultimate Auto," he told Smerb. "You might as well go back to your hotel."

"I can't," said Smerb. "It's too much money, and I've only got enough left to buy the vitamins for the dog pound."

"Well, in that case, you can stay at my home," said Madia.

"Thank you," Smerb said. "That takes care of my problem."

"You may not believe it," said Madia, "but there are a lot of people with bigger problems than yours."

There were indeed! Riders in taxis all over the city were slowly going broke. Ice-cream trucks ran out of ice, and the people in the white suits had to give away their ice cream free. The fish in Mr. Kraken's truck had rotted, and people were walking around holding their noses.

School buses could not move either, so all city schools were closed. It was awful!

That evening the mayor appeared again on television. This time Smerb watched from Officer Madia's house as the mayor stated that the Ultimate Auto had not yet been found.

"However, we are still doing everything in our power to get things moving again. As one more step, I have ordered that all traffic lights stop flashing red. Now all cars in the city have a green light to go, uh, when they get a chance. Finally, you may be pleased to know that I have just fired the head of the New York City police."

Smerb clapped for the mayor. "But," he said to his four-footed friends, "we are still stuck here! Might as well try to make the best of it until this mess clears up."

The next morning, Smerb took his dogs and Madia's five boys to the zoo. They all had a good time. But there was one thing wrong. They couldn't hear the lions roar, or the seals bark, or the snakes hiss. They couldn't even hear themselves talk. There was just too much noise from the helicopters, the planes, and the car horns in the crowded streets around the zoo.

By the end of the day, the overworked police officers had decided that the Ultimate Auto was not in the east, nor in the west, nor in the south of the city. That night the mayor went on television again to tell the people that they were now looking only in the north and the center of the city.

Smerb was watching the mayor with the Madias—all eight of them, even Grandma. He was happy staying with them. So were his four-footed friends and the Madia boys, who played together like old friends.

At dinner, everyone talked about the Ultimate Auto. For the first time, Smerb told everyone what had happened to *him* as he rounded the corner at Forty-Second Street and Fifth Avenue.

"*What!*" said Officer Madia, his tired face looking bright once more. "*Say that again!*"

"I pulled in between the truck and the bus. Then I stopped, and the taxi behind me stopped. I was crowded in like a key in a lock. Say, why are you turning green?"

Madia jumped to the phone and quickly called the mayor's special number.

"I may be wrong," he said, turning to Smerb, "and I may get fired, but I'm going to tell the mayor that the Ultimate Auto is *yours.*"

Smerb fainted. So did his four-footed friends.

Part Three
The Ultimate Answer

On the following day, the action around the Ultimate Auto was not to be believed. Officer Madia was there with his family. The mayor was there, and so were the heads of traffic and police, who were now back on their jobs. A crowd of about ten thousand was also there. So were about one hundred television people, their cameras and microphones working away. Of course, Samuel Smerb was there, too, with his four-footed friends.

Suddenly, every camera, every microphone, and every face turned toward Smerb. "I just want to say," said Smerb, "that I'm here only because we ran out of Vitamin Z at the dog pound. I'm from the Lincoln Animal Society upstate, and so are my four-footed friends here. New York is a nice place to visit, but I don't like to drive here."

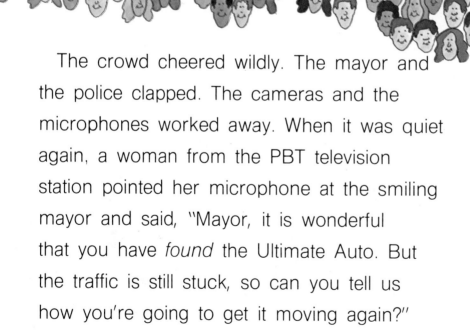

The crowd cheered wildly. The mayor and the police clapped. The cameras and the microphones worked away. When it was quiet again, a woman from the PBT television station pointed her microphone at the smiling mayor and said, "Mayor, it is wonderful that you have *found* the Ultimate Auto. But the traffic is still stuck, so can you tell us how you're going to get it moving again?"

The mayor's smile fell at her feet and broke into little pieces. She scratched her head for a minute, and then turned to the secretary of traffic control. "I think you can answer that, eh, Bob?"

The secretary of traffic control stopped smiling, too. He scratched his ear, and then he turned to the head of the police. "This seems to be your job, eh, Charlie?"

The smile of the head of the city police disappeared behind his handkerchief as he loudly blew his nose. Finally, he turned to Officer Madia. "Well, Mr. Madia, you *found* the Ultimate Auto. Now what are you going to do about the traffic jam?"

Madia couldn't reach for his handkerchief or scratch his head since two of his boys were holding his hands. He licked his lips for a minute, then he turned to the PBT woman and said, "Uh…I…well…you see… maybe…it's—"

But before Madia could finish what he was about to say, that angry taxi driver jumped in front of the cameras and microphones and, still shaking his fist at Smerb, said, "If it were up to me, I'd take this man's Ultimate Auto and break it up into little pieces and—"

"And mail the pieces back to Smerb," said Officer Madia. "I was just about to say that if we take the Ultimate Auto apart, then the traffic can move again. It's as easy as taking a key out of a lock."

The crowd cheered. The mayor and her people clapped. The microphones and the cameras worked away. Only Smerb didn't seem pleased.

"Look," he told everyone, "you can mail the pieces of my car back to me. That'll be fine. But I've still got to pick up those vitamins and get back to the dog pound. How do I do *that?*"

"Why, in my police helicopter," the mayor said quickly.

At that, the crowd cheered and clapped.

That sounds like the end of the story, but it isn't. Smerb did get the Vitamin Z, and he did get back to the Lincoln Animal Society in upstate New York, and the mayor let him keep the helicopter until all the pieces of the Ultimate Auto had been sent in the mail.

But somebody had made a mistake. Part of the car was sent to a Samuel Smerb of the Lincoln Animal Society in upstate *New Mexico.* When the real Smerb told the mayor this, there was only one thing the mayor could do.

"Okay," she said, "you can *keep* my helicopter. But do one thing for me."

"Sure," said Smerb.

"Stay out of town," the mayor roared. "Just stay out of town."

Smerb does just that. If you ever get up to the Lincoln Animal Society, you may see him. When he isn't working at the dog pound, Smerb still takes his four-footed friends for rides. Now he does it in a real New York City police helicopter. Sometimes Officer Madia and the boys go along, too.

A hippo yawned

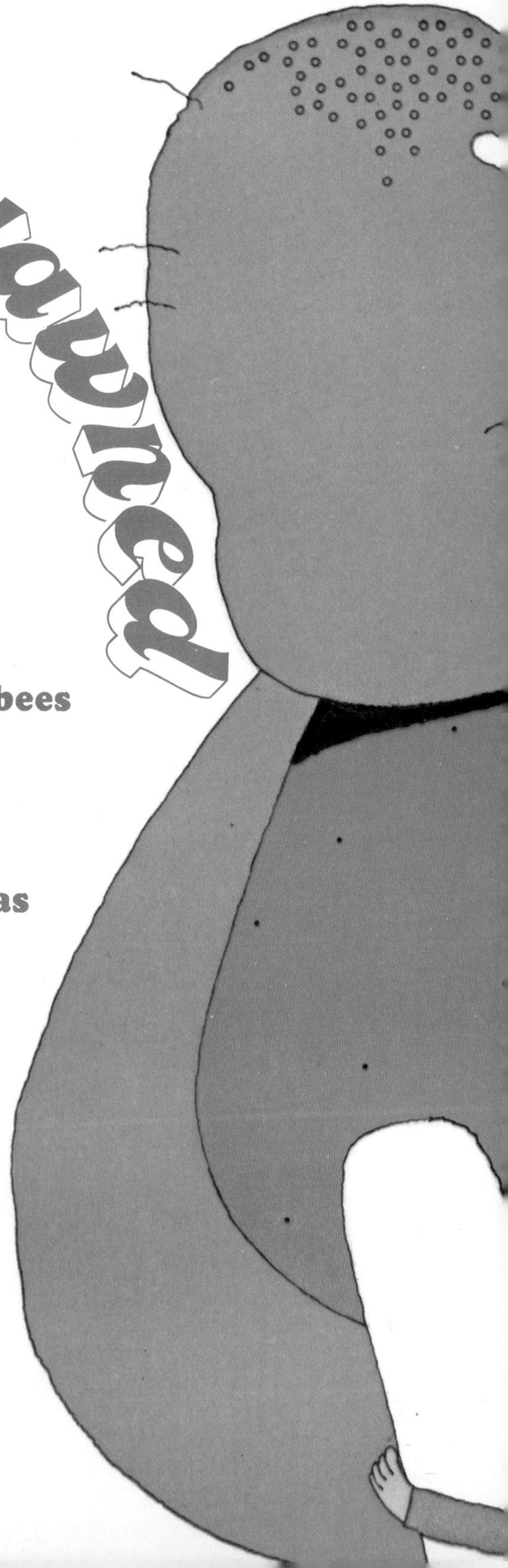

A hippo yawned
And I looked inside
And saw three monkeys
Taking a ride.
Then one of them yawned
And I looked inside
And there were three bumble bees
Taking a ride.
Then one of them yawned
And I looked inside
And there were three little fleas
Taking a ride.
Then one of them yawned
And I looked inside
And there were three hippos
Taking a ride.

— Arnold Spilka

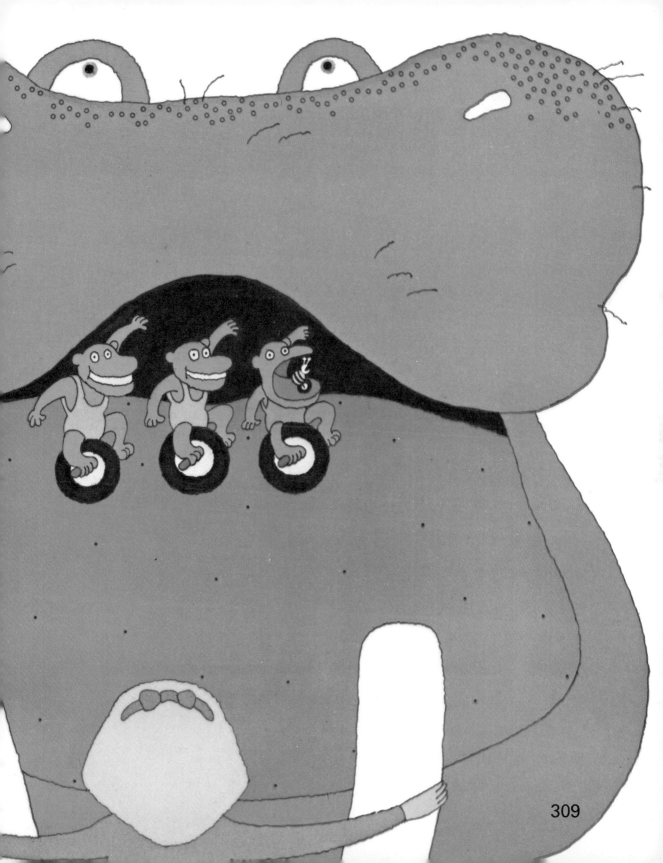

THE GREAT FISH

Peter Parnall

Charlie sat at his grandfather's feet, enjoying the warmth of the old cabin. Outside, a cold wind blew. Just minutes before, as he had been walking there, the frosty breeze had made his nose and hands numb.

Now he sat on the floor, feeling very safe, surrounded by familiar things.

It was the time of year when yellow leaves dipped and bucked through the

air. Charlie could hear them scraping against the walls of the cabin. It was the time of year when dry cornstalks chattered, and the air was heavy with the smell of fermenting apples.

It was the time of year when the deer and the bear crept by night into the fields and became fat on the wastes of the harvest.

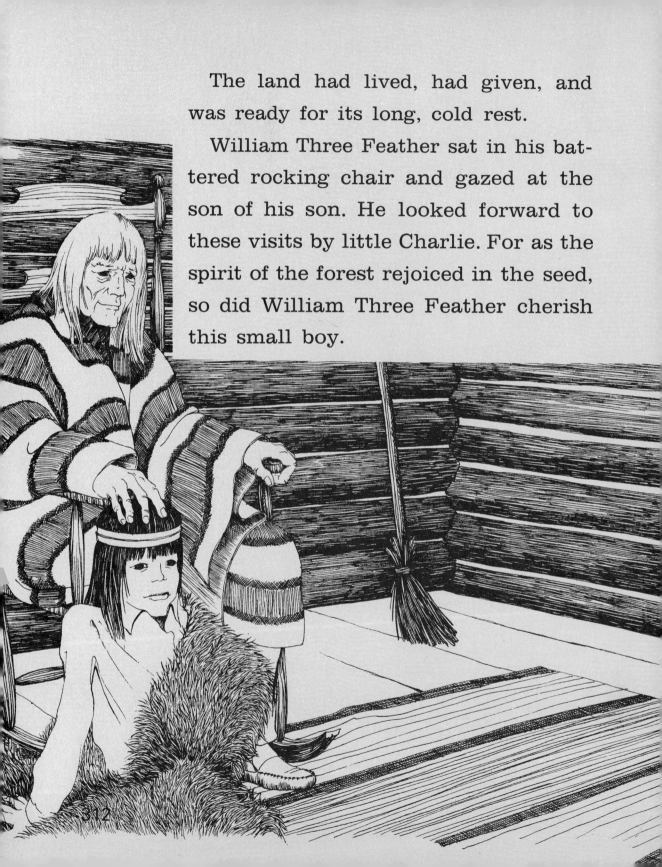

The land had lived, had given, and was ready for its long, cold rest.

William Three Feather sat in his battered rocking chair and gazed at the son of his son. He looked forward to these visits by little Charlie. For as the spirit of the forest rejoiced in the seed, so did William Three Feather cherish this small boy.

Charlie's eyes roamed the walls of the cabin where his grandfather's things hung—things that had stories to tell. There were many furs. There were snowshoes and a battered old rifle that was rusting its usefulness away.

On the walls and floor were rugs made from bark and the wool of wild mountain sheep. These rugs could keep out the rain and the winds of winter. One rug hanging by the wood stove told the story of Three Feather's ancestors. Leaning against the wall was a long pole tipped with bone: a salmon spear.

Charlie had heard many stories from the old man: the tale of the Great Elk of the West Mountain, the tale of the Winter, when the wolves lost their fear of people, and the tale of the Night Demon Owl.

Best of all he liked to hear tales of his people and how they lived with the eagle, the bear, the water, and the forest.

Charlie's eyes fell on the spear once more. He said, "Grandfather, tell me again of the great silver salmon."

Three Feather smiled. "The ruler of the fish, the friend of our people." He closed his eyes and began to rock. It helped him remember.

"When the spring sun smiled and broke the grip of the river ice, the storerooms were nearly bare, and the people grew thin. There was great hunger.

"The children were weak. The tears of the mothers were carried by the river waters to the sea. The great salmon wondered at these drops of water that were salty like the ocean. They had never seen such water flow from the land. They wondered and began to swim toward the mountains where the river was born.

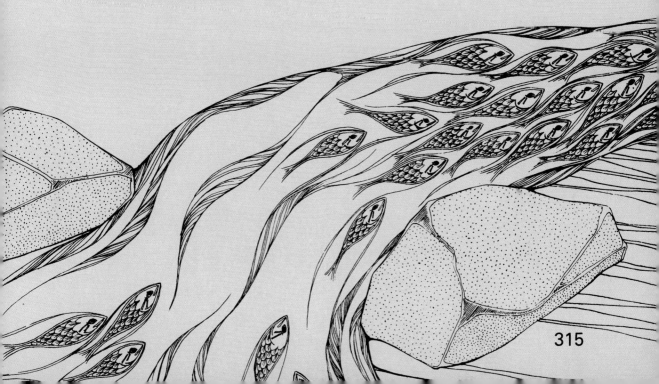

"Even as the cries of the mothers pierced the air, schools of salmon began to choke the river mouth. The water gave way to flesh, so great were the numbers of fish that swam toward our mountains.

"No obstacle was too great for them. They leaped the highest waterfall and conquered the swiftest rapid. As they swam, the sounds of their coming were heard at the farthest long house.

"The braves gathered traps and spears and stood by the river, staring in awe as the salmon swam into the shallows. They were as many as rocks in the riverbed.

"The sun shone bright and gave strength to the hunger-weakened braves. Three days and three nights they stayed, scooping the fat silver fish from the water. When the fourth sun rose, the storerooms were full. The cries

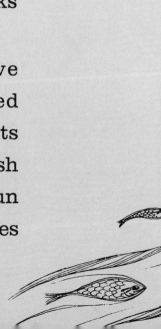

of the children stopped, and the mothers smiled once more.

"Since that time, the great fish has never failed us. It grew to love the clean waters of our mountains and chose to bring forth its children here.

"The Great Fish loved the sun and the sparkling gravel, as do our people. It loved to hunt and move in the waters, as do our people. It loved the clean sight and smell of the waters, as do our people. It loved the Earth, as do our people."

William Three Feather rose, moving stiffly. He picked up the spear. His eyes watered as he said, "I know this tale to be true, little Charlie, for I have seen the hoards of silver fish. I have helped catch and store them to keep our people strong." Slowly he replaced the spear.

"But now, my son, even a mother's tears are not enough."

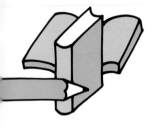

As Wise As an Owl

Sometimes words don't really mean what they say. You have to read all the words in the sentence. Then you will know what the words really mean. Read this sentence.

Max is as wise as an owl.

There is no way you can know how wise an owl really is. People say they *think* owls look wise. Max always seems to know the right answer. So Max *seems* to be wise.

Now read each numbered sentence. Choose an answer that tells the real meaning of that sentence. Write the answer on your paper.

1. Mary finishes a job as quick as a wink.
   Mary has beautiful blue eyes.
   Mary takes all day to do a job.
   Mary does a job very quickly.

2. That bed is as hard as a rock.
   That bed is very soft.
   That bed is not soft in any way.
   That bed is full of stones.

3. The room looks like an earthquake hit it.
   The room is certainly a mess.
   The room is too small.
   The room is very clean and neat.

4. After I won, I was walking on a cloud.
   After I won, I was very angry.
   After I won, I was very happy.
   After I won, I was very sad.

5. Allen was as busy as a bee.
   Allen was working to get his jobs done.
   Allen was flying around making honey.
   Allen was thinking of going to bed.

6. The wind howled through the trees.
   The wind sang a folk song.
   The wind in the trees made lots of noise.
   The wind blew its horn like a truck.

7. The sun smiled down at me on the beach.
   The sun burned my skin.
   The sun was covered by clouds.
   The sun at the beach was bright and warm.

ORIGAMI

Elinor Tripato Massoglia

Origami is the Japanese art of paper folding. No one knows when it began. But today, people all over the world enjoy doing origami.

In origami, paper is folded to make a shape. You can make people, animals, fish, and many other shapes.

Before you start to make a shape, there are some things you need to know.

1. Always work on a hard table.
2. Follow the directions carefully.
3. Use paper that folds easily.
4. Be sure your paper is square.
5. Lift the paper off the table only when the directions tell you to lift it.
6. Use both hands. Hold the paper with your fingers.
7. Use your thumbs to crease the folds. Always crease the folds hard.

Now you are ready to begin. Find a piece of paper with straight sides. To make sure your paper is square, look at these pictures. Read the directions and follow each step carefully.

1.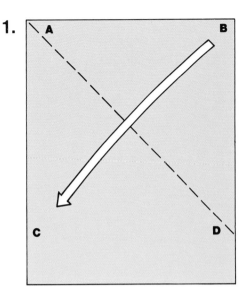

Fold your paper so that Side A-B lies on top of Side A-C.

2.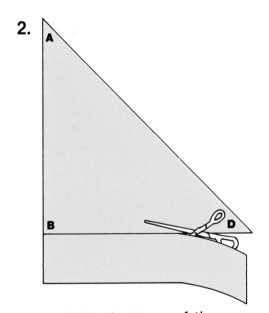

Cut off the bottom of the paper from Corner D to Corner B.

3.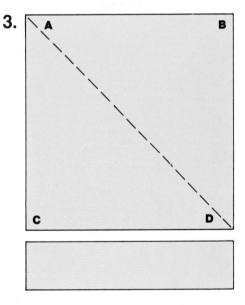

Unfold your paper and you will have a square, A-B-C-D. Put the leftover paper aside.

Here is a shape you can make with your paper square.

1.

Fold your paper so that Side A-B lies on top of Side A-C. Now open your paper. There should be a crease from Corner A to Corner D.

2.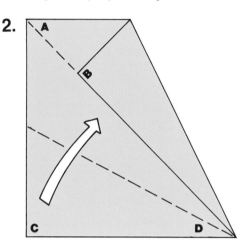

Fold the corners, B and C, so they meet in the middle of the paper on the crease.

3.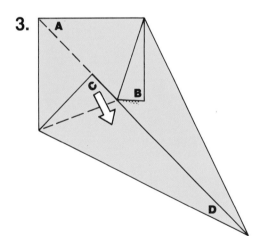

Fold the corners, B and C, back just a little, the way they are shown in this picture.

4.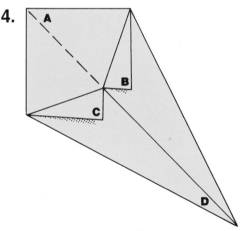

Your paper should look like this. Now lift it up and turn it over.

324

5.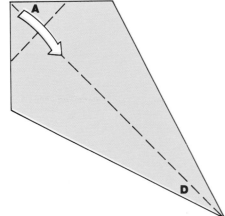

Fold Corner A down, just a little.

6.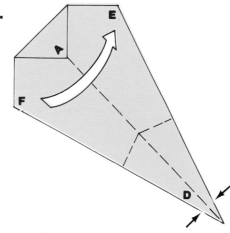

Now look at this picture carefully. Pinch Corner D with your fingers and lift it up toward Corner A. At the same time, use your other hand to fold Corner F to Corner E.

7.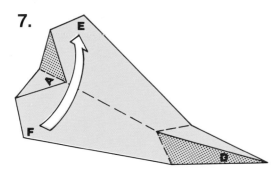

This is how the shape looks when it is partly folded.

8.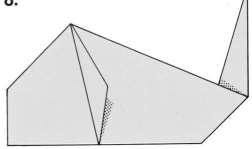

This is how it looks when it is finished. You have folded a fish!

Here is another shape you can make with your paper square.

1.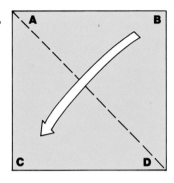

Fold your paper so that Side A-B lies on top of Side A-C. Turn the paper so that Corner B is at the top.

2.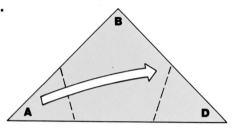

Fold Corner A up so that it lies halfway between Corner B and Corner D.

3.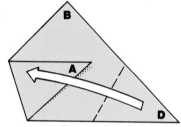

Fold Corner D so that it lies on top of folded Corner A.

5.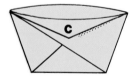

Your cup is finished! Open the center between Corners B and C. Fill the cup and have a drink of water.

4.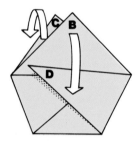

Fold Corner B down over folded Corners A and D. Lift the paper and turn it over. Fold down Corner C.

Answers

The Case of the Whistling Ghost

Encyclopedia Brown knew that Rocky had made up "the other boy." Another boy could not have run "out the back door and into the woods" with the stolen camera, as Rocky said.

Do you remember that Fabius wanted to take a picture of a spider web? The web was spun "across the bottom half" of the back door. Had "the other boy" really run out the back door, he would have broken the web!

Hit and Run

There were three players on each team.

Growing Time

Sandol Stoddard Warburg

Part One
Jamie and King

Jamie lives in a big old house in the country. There are apple trees and cherry trees, grapes and wild roses all around the house. The back porch is starting to fall down, but Granny always says the way those roses are climbing, they'll hold it up another hundred years. It is a good house to live in, warm inside and full of happiness.

King is Jamie's dog. King is so old now that he sleeps most of the time in the kitchen, by the stove where it is warm. All day he sleeps there on his old red blanket, and sometimes he dreams, and groans in his sleep.

When Jamie was very little, just learning to stand up, it was King who stood beside him and taught him how to walk. Jamie would sink his fingers deep into King's soft, woolly, golden coat and hang on tightly while King walked very carefully, step by step across the kitchen floor. After a while, Jamie only needed to hold on with one hand. At last, he learned to walk by himself, and then he followed King everywhere.

In the spring they explored the farm, and Jamie learned how to run and to jump. In the summer they played at the pond together, and if Jamie went in too far, King would pull him out again. In the fall they played in great red and golden piles of fallen leaves. They ran in circles together, trying to catch the leaves that floated down from the trees, before they touched the ground.

Now winter has come and gone, and other winters and other summers, too. Jamie now knows how to climb fences and how to climb trees, and he has just learned to skip stones on the pond. But now that Jamie can do all these things, King doesn't want to come with him any more. King is too old and tired. His legs hurt him, and his teeth are nearly gone. He just wants to lie by the stove and be quiet.

The time of King's life is nearly over now. His time is spent sleeping and dreaming. When he groans in his sleep and thumps his tail on the floor, he is remembering all the good old times, all the funny and sad and happy and wonderful days of his long, long life.

One morning Jamie wakes up quite early and sees his mother coming into the room. She sits down beside his bed, and her face is very sad.

"I must tell you something, Jamie," she says, "and I am so sorry because it is something that makes us all feel very unhappy. King is dead."

"Why is King dead? Where is he?" Jamie asks, and he begins to cry. Always and always, King has been there waiting for Jamie down in the kitchen every morning. Even when he was very old, he still wanted to lick Jamie's face. He still thumped his tired old tail on the floor.

Jamie's mother talks to him for a long time. Jamie sees tears in her eyes, too. "It is better for King," she says. "He is happy now. His teeth don't hurt him anymore."

"But I want King," says Jamie. "I don't want him to go away from me, ever."

"I know," answers his mother. "It hurts very badly to lose King, and it will not stop hurting right away. Daddy and I will help you all we can. Later, we will go to see King's grave under the apple trees on the hill. We will plant some flowers there for him."

When Jamie comes into the kitchen for breakfast, Granny is sitting in the corner listening to her little radio, doing her knitting. She is making a red hat for Jamie, and she has it almost finished now. She looks at him, and for a moment Jamie thinks she is going to say something, but then she doesn't. She just smiles at him and goes on with her knitting. In a little while, she turns off her radio and fixes a sandwich for Jamie. But he does not want to eat it.

All day long, Jamie stays quiet in the kitchen near Granny. He is pretending to play with his old yellow truck, but he is not really playing. He is just pushing the truck slowly back and forth while he thinks about King. The warm sun creeps quietly across the kitchen floor while Jamie remembers all the days when King was still alive. Each day is like a picture to him, clear and perfect as if it were happening all over again, right now.

The day when King was chasing yellow butterflies round and round, barking and barking...

The day King went to sleep in the sun and a fat hen climbed up on his back and went to sleep, too...

The day Jamie's friends came to swim in the pond and King was angry because it was HIS pond. He didn't want a lot of people jumping around in it...

The day King tried to make friends with a skunk...

The day Jamie got lost in the woods and it was getting dark, but King was there and King showed him the way back home...

And there are so many days to remember that Jamie is thinking all afternoon while the sun goes down. And Granny rocks and rocks in her old chair beside the window. Finally Jamie looks at the old red blanket by the stove, and he says to Granny, "King doesn't need his blanket anymore."

Then she tells him to sit beside her in the rocking chair and keep her company. Jamie rests his head on Granny's shoulder, and together they watch the sun going down behind the apple trees, below the dark and shining rim of the hill.

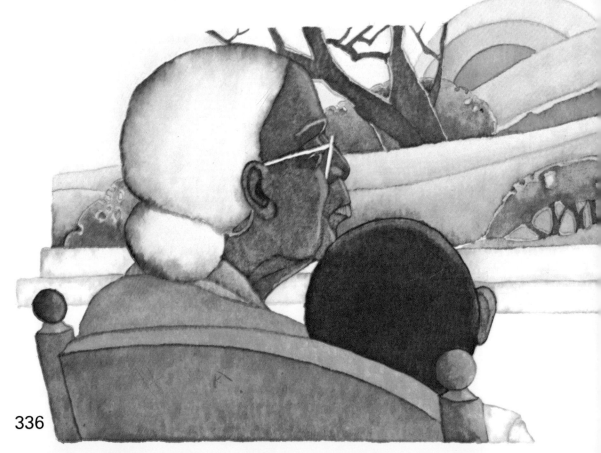

"I want King to come back, Granny," says Jamie. But he knows that King will not come back, ever again. Granny stops rocking the chair and stares at him, then gives her head a little shake.

"Come back?" she says. "Why Jamie, where on earth do you think King has gone to?"

"I know where he has gone. Because he is dead. He is under the apple trees, on the hill. Uncle John put him there."

"Oh, child, listen to you," says Granny. "What's down there under the apple trees is nothing to King anymore. That's only his poor worn-out body that was nothing but aches and pains to him."

She begins rocking again. "Nothing but aches and pains," she says. "Poor King, and you sitting here not using your head at all. Look here, there was more to King than four tired old legs and some yellow fur. You know that. We named him King when he was a pup, not just because of his pretty coat, but because of the spirit that was in him. He was that kind of a dog. He had the spirit of a king."

"Uncle John says the spirit is gone from King now."

"And that's the truth. But where has it gone to? Did you think of that? It couldn't be in the ground, you know. That's not where it belongs. Has King's spirit got no home to come to anymore?"

Jamie looks again at the old red blanket, resting so small and quiet by the stove. "King's home is with me," he says, "right here."

"Of course, it is," says Granny. "That's what I'm talking about. And that's where King has been today, right here with you and me. That's where he is right now."

"No. You're pretending. You're trying to fool me, Granny."

"Don't be silly," snaps Granny, taking off her glasses. "You know when I'm fooling and when I'm not fooling, better than that. You say *no* because you can't see King anymore. Well, look here, child, I can't see a thing without my glasses. I can't see the stove over there, but I know where it is, all right. I can't even see my shoes right now, but I know my feet are in them, don't I? Well, I know what's in my heart, too. And I know King still has a home to come to."

"Were you thinking about King all that time, too, Granny?"

"Not thinking, really. Just letting him keep me company."

"I was, too."

"I know you were. I could see that, too, without looking. When you're as old as I am, Jamie, you won't count on your eyes so much. You'll count on your heart more. So remember this, child: the spirit of something you really love can never die. It lives in your heart. It belongs to you always."

"I will remember. I. will never forget King."

"I don't expect you will. But as you grow up, let your heart grow bigger, too. Your young heart is like a warm, snug little house, you see, where you can keep all that is most important in life to you. Well then, fill your house, child. And when it is filled, add more rooms to it. Always make more and more rooms in that little house of yours, until it is big as it can be. Store up your riches there."

Jamie doesn't say anything. He is thinking about King running about the farm, King chasing the yellow butterflies, the golden leaves. Granny is rocking again now, singing an old, old tune. Jamie listens. He can remember that Granny used to sing that same song for him when she rocked him on the back porch when he was a baby.

"I remember that song, Granny, from when I was a baby."

"So do I. Don't forget, I was a baby once, too. I remember my mother, rocking me and singing that very same song. Goodness knows where it comes from, that song is so old."

"I guess you are very, very old, aren't you, Granny?" Jamie asks. "Are you going to die soon?"

"Not tonight, I'm not," says Granny. "Tonight I've got to cook meatballs and biscuits."

Part Two

A New Beginning

"Where's Mama?" asks Jamie.

"Mama and Uncle John went off in the truck."

"Where did they go? And why couldn't I go with them?"

"Because you were busy here with me. You had things to think about." Granny's fingers are patting out the biscuit dough. "Come along now, make yourself useful. I'll get the meatballs started; you cut the biscuits for me."

"I'm hungry," says Jamie, cutting biscuits. "Where did Mama and Uncle John go?"

"To meet your Daddy. They are bringing something home for you."

"What?"

"A surprise."

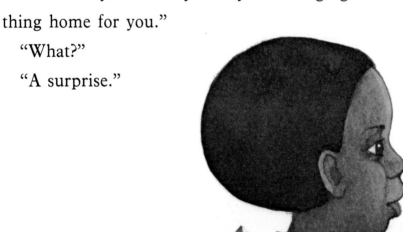

Soon Jamie hears the truck turning into the driveway. Jamie runs out to the porch.

"Wait inside, Jamie," calls his father.

Soon Daddy comes in carrying something in a covered basket, with Mama close behind him. He puts the basket in the middle of the kitchen floor, and smiles at Jamie. Uncle John comes in, too, wiping his boots on the doormat and looking pleased. Granny comes over by the basket. All of them are standing there, looking at Jamie, smiling.

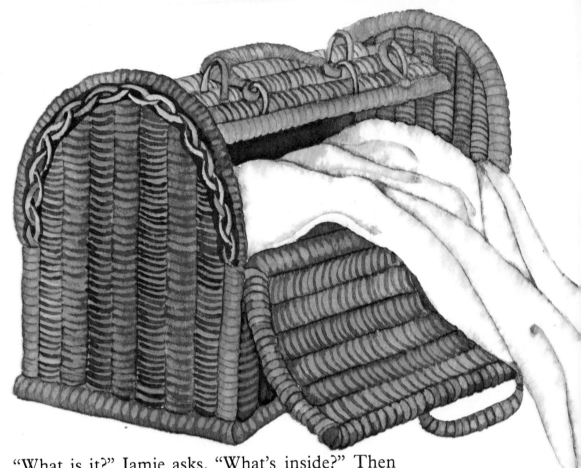

"What is it?" Jamie asks. "What's inside?" Then
he hears a tiny noise, something like a bark, but
not quite. Now the basket is shaking, and Jamie
hears the noise again, a little louder this time.

As they watch, two very small brown paws
come poking over the rim of the basket. The
lid is pushed up by a little brown head with long,
soft ears. Two bright brown eyes stare at Jamie for
a second, then the lid goes down. There is a
squeaking and a struggling in the bottom of the
basket again.

344

Daddy's big laugh booms out, and soon they are all beginning to laugh. Uncle John reaches down into the basket and lifts out a ball of soft brown fur, not much bigger than one of Jamie's shoes. Carefully, he places the ball on the kitchen floor. "Well, hello there," he says, "how are you doing?" The ball stretches out four tiny legs and stands up for a second, then flops down on the floor and squeaks.

"Is that a dog?" asks Jamie. "Is that really a dog?"

"Well," Uncle John answers, looking sideways at Jamie, "you might say it's not much of a dog right now. But give him some growing time. He's going to be quite a dog."

"Big as King?"

"Different from King," his father says. "Bigger, maybe. It's hard to tell right now just how he's going to turn out."

"Isn't he a beauty, though?" says Mama happily.

The puppy stands up again barking his squeaky little bark. He is wagging his tail so hard that his back legs are sliding around in circles on the floor. Then he falls down again.

"He doesn't even know how to walk," says Jamie. Suddenly Jamie feels so lonely and miserable about King again that he goes over by himself, and sits down in the corner by the stove. He begins rolling his old truck back and forth again. He does not want to look at the new dog. He does not want to look at anyone. "King, King," he thinks to himself. "I don't want anyone but you, ever. Not ever!"

It is time for supper, and Jamie eats everything on his plate without saying a word. He helps to clear the table, and then he goes up to his room. He does not go near the new puppy again. He does not even say good-night to his father, or to his mother, or to Granny or Uncle John.

"Jamie?" His father is calling him. He comes into Jamie's room and sits down beside the bed. Jamie turns his face away. "Believe me, Jamie, I do know how you feel," says his father, "and I am sorry about it." Then his father talks for a long time about King. But Jamie will not listen; he is counting the cracks in the wall. After a while, his father says again, "I'm sorry," and he adds, "Maybe it was the wrong thing to do, bringing the new puppy home so soon. He doesn't have to stay, if you don't want him. Mama and I will understand if you say no. It's up to you." He says good-night to Jamie and goes out, closing the door behind him.

Then Jamie lies in the dark, hearing the footsteps and the voices in the house growing quieter and quieter until the last door has closed, and suddenly he knows that he is asleep. Then very slowly he begins to have a wonderful dream. He dreams that in the dark he can hear the roses growing and blooming and the beans and corn coming up in the garden. The sound they make is warm and sweet as a summer wind, like the sound of Granny's singing that goes round and round forever.

After a time he can hear each plant putting out its leaves and its fruit, each one singing its own small tune alone.

And all this time Jamie dreams that he is lying warm in a bed of golden grass. The moon goes slowly over and the stars shine on and on. Toward morning, Jamie begins to notice another sound, nearer to him. It is a sound as if the heart of the earth were beating its own sure and easy time, not hurrying, just being there with him, and promising to stay with him forever. Close by his ear now, that slow soft thump-thumping is a promise so dear to Jamie, that he begins to smile in his sleep. "Hello, King," he says, still dreaming, but he is beginning to wake up at last. He feels himself smiling and hears himself saying, "Hello" in his own room.

THUMP-CLANK! Suddenly, there is a louder noise, and Jamie is awake. He sits up in his bed. The moon has fallen below the rim of the hill now, and the sky is pale with early morning light. CLANK! Something is happening in the kitchen. Jamie gets out of bed and tiptoes down the stairs. He leans around the corner and looks into the kitchen, but at first he can't see anything. Then in a dim corner of the room, he hears a tiny scratching noise. Jamie turns on the light by the kitchen stove.

"Oh, look at you!" he says to the new puppy.
"Look what you've done! You're a mess!" The puppy
has climbed out of his box by the stove. He has
been playing with King's red blanket, and he has
scattered scraps of paper all over the kitchen floor.
Two empty milk bottles by the back door are
knocked over. King's water dish is upside down,
and the new puppy has had a cold swim in the
drinking water by mistake. He is lying in a pool of
water, shivering and crying. Every time he tries to
creep away, his paws slide in the water. He falls
down and begins to cry again.

Jamie picks up King's blanket. "Well," he tells
the puppy, "I guess I'll just have to take care of
you." He takes the shivering puppy in his arms
and warms him in King's old blanket. The puppy
is frightened at first; Jamie has to hold him tight,
so he won't slide out.

Together they sit down in Granny's chair by the window, and they watch the sky turn bright and golden as the sun comes up. The birds are singing and hopping in the grass. The mist is rising from the pond. "You are too small yet to have a name," says Jamie to the puppy. "You need some growing time. I guess I'll wait and see what kind of a puppy you are. Then I'll think of a good name for you."

The puppy is quiet now. He is warm in the rocking chair with Jamie. He cocks his little head and listens carefully to everything Jamie says. Jamie talks to him for a long time. The puppy listens and watches Jamie with his bright little eyes, waiting to see what will happen next.

Where Does the Butterfly Go When It Rains?

May Garelick

Rain. Rain. Rain. Rain.
Where does the butterfly go
when it rains?

And the mole and the bee
and the bird in the tree—
where do they go when it rains?

A mole can stay in his hole.
A bee can fly back to her hive.

I've heard that a bird
tucks its head under its wing.

But where does the butterfly go
when it rains?

I know that my cat goes scat
under the porch.
I've seen him do that when it rains.

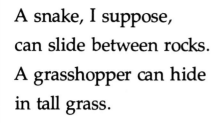

A snake, I suppose,
can slide between rocks.
A grasshopper can hide
in tall grass.

A rabbit can dash—
whoosh—into a bush.

But where does the butterfly go
when it rains?

The cows I see in the field
just stand in the rain and get wet.
They eat and get wet
and eat and get wetter.
Don't cows mind the rain?

I know why a duck doesn't mind the rain.
Someone told me.
A duck's feathers are oily and slick,
so the rain doesn't stick.
Water slides off a duck's back.
Quack! Quack!

But what about minnows
and how about trout?
Where do fish go when it rains?

Pooh! That's silly.
It doesn't rain under water.

What does a turtle do in the rain?
If I were a turtle with a shell over me,
I would know what to do
in the rain, wouldn't you?

But what can a butterfly do?
How can it fly if its wings are wet?
Where does the butterfly go
when it rains?

And the bird in the tree
is a puzzle to me.
Even if its head is tucked
under its wing,
what happens to the rest of it,
poor thing?

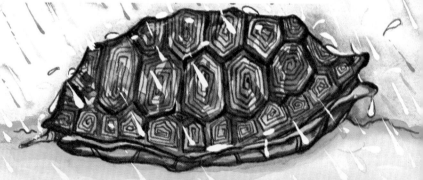

As soon as the rain
stops raining so hard,
I'll go quietly up to a tree.
And maybe I'll find
a bird in that tree,
and I'll see what it does in the rain.

Maybe I'll find a butterfly, too.
Then I'll know what *it* does
when it rains.

But where can I look?
I've never seen a butterfly
out in the rain.
Have you?

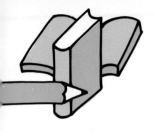

People and Places

Words that name special people, places, or things must begin with capital letters. When you write, you sometimes use a person's name or the name of a special place or a special thing. Then, the names of these special people, places, or things must begin with capital letters.

Read the sentence below. Which words name special people, places, or things?

Ben walks down Main Street to Hill School.

Ben is the name of a person. *Main Street* is the name of a special place — a street. *Hill School* is the special name of something — a school. All these names begin with capital letters.

Now read the sentences on the next page. In each sentence, find the word or words that name special people, places, or things. Then write the sentence correctly on your paper.

1. Today, anita bought a book from mr. allen.

   1. Today, Anita bought a book from Mr. Allen.

2. Let's invite tom and suzy to the party.

3. We went swimming in the pacific ocean.

4. Aunt ann brought me a present from boston.

5. Is alaska bigger than texas?

6. Last month, I visited a friend who lives in Los angeles, california.

7. We met everett on hernandez street.

8. Miyoko played music by bach and handel.

9. Roberto clemente played ball for the pittsburgh pirates.

10. The parade passed by uncle walter's house.

11. My friend sam now lives in hawaii.

12. We saw raul riding his new bike along third street.

13. Two famous artists were picasso and mary cassatt.

14. Did you go to charles street when you were in boston?

15. Pam and her family are on a trip to south america.

ENDINGS

It can make you feel very good when you find a way to deal with a hard problem. The answer may be so easy that you want to laugh. The answer to a hard problem may surprise you, too.

Thinking About "Endings"

1. Why did Dr. Naismith invent the game of basketball?
2. How did Encyclopedia Brown know that Rocky took the camera?
3. What things happened that told the photographer where Russet might live?
4. How did the people of Boston help Mrs. Mallard find an answer to her problem?
5. Why do you think Jamie's mother, father, and uncle bought a new puppy for Jamie?
6. What are some ways you have found to deal with hard problems?

Glossary

This glossary will help you to pronounce and to understand the meanings of some of the unusual or difficult words in this book.

The pronunciation of each word is printed beside the word in this way: **o·pen** (ō′pən). The letters, signs, and key words in the list below will help you read the pronunciation respelling. When an entry word has more than one syllable, a dark accent mark (′) is placed after the syllable that has the heaviest stress. In some words, a light accent mark (′) is placed after the syllable that receives a less heavy stress.

The pronunciation key, syllable breaks, accent mark placements, and phonetic respellings in this glossary are adapted from the Macmillan *Beginning Dictionary* (1981) and the Macmillan *School Dictionary* (1981). Other dictionaries may use other pronunciation symbols.

Pronunciation Key

a	bad	**hw**	white	**ô**	off	**th**	that	ə	*stands for*
ā	cake	**i**	it	**oo**	wood	**u**	cup	a	*as in* ago
ä	father	**ī**	ice	**ōo**	food	**ur**	turn	e	*as in* taken
b	bat	**j**	joke	**oi**	oil	**yōo**	music	i	*as in* pencil
ch	chin	**k**	kit	**ou**	out	**v**	very	o	*as in* lemon
d	dog	**l**	lid	**p**	pail	**w**	wet	u	*as in* helpful
e	pet	**m**	man	**r**	ride	**y**	yes		
ē	me	**n**	not	**s**	sit	**z**	zoo		
f	five	**ng**	sing	**sh**	ship	**zh**	treasure		
g	game	**o**	hot	**t**	tall				
h	hit	**ō**	open	**th**	thin				

A

a·bil·i·ty (ə bil′ə tē) *n.*   talent or skill.

ache (āk) *n.*   continuous, usually dull, pain.

a·cre (ā′kər) *n.*   a measure of land equal to 43,560 square feet.

ac·tu·al·ly (ak′chσō ə lē) *adv.* in fact; really.

ad·mir·er (ad mīr′ər) *n.*   a person who thinks someone or something is very good or very beautiful.

a·gen·cy (ā′jən sē) *n. pl.,* **a·gen·cies.**   a company or person that has the power to do business for others.

an·ces·tor (an′ses′tər) *n.*   a person from whom one is descended.

ar·rive (ə rīv′) *v.* **ar·rived, ar·riv·ing.**   to reach a place by traveling; to come.

at·tach (ə tach′) *v.*   to fasten to or on; join; connect.

au·to (ô′tō) *n.*   a shortened form of automobile; car.

av·e·nue (av′ə nyōō′, av′ə nōō′) *n.*   a wide street.

awe (ô) *n.*   great wonder together with fear or deep respect.

B

ba·nan·a (bə nan′ə) *n.*   a slightly curved fruit that has yellow or red skin.

bar·gain (bär′gin) *n.*   something worth more than the price paid for it.

bar·rel (bar′əl) *n.*   a large wooden container shaped like a cylinder, usually made of boards held together by metal hoops.

bean·curd (bēn′curd′) *n.*   pressed, puréed soybeans, usually sold in white, custardlike squares, and eaten extensively in the Orient.

beck·on (bek′ən) *v.*   to make a sign or signal to someone.

bee·hive (bē′hīv′) *n.*   a hive or house for a colony of bees.

bi·cy·cle (bī′si kəl) *n.*   a light vehicle to ride on. A bicycle has two wheels, one behind the other; a seat; handlebars; and two foot pedals.

bis·cuit (bis′kit) *n.*   a small, quick bread made from dough.

booth (bōōth) *n.*   a stall for the display or sale of goods.

bor · der (bôr′dər) *n.* a boundary line.

breeze (brēz) *n.* a soft, gentle wind.

bur · row (bur′ō) *v.* to dig a hole in which to live or hide.

bush (boosh) *n. pl.,* **bush · es.** a woody plant or shrub.

C

calm (käm) *adj.* free from excitement or strong feeling; quiet; serene.

cam · er · a (kam′ər ə, kam′rə) *n.* a device for taking photographs or motion pictures.

cap · i · tal (kap′i təl) *adj.* (of an alphabetic letter) of a form different from and higher than its corresponding lowercase letter, as A, B, Q, R.

Car · ni · val (kär′nə vəl) *n.* the period of feasting and merrymaking that comes just before Lent.

car · riage (kar′ij) *n.* a wheeled vehicle for transporting people, usually drawn by a horse or horses.

cer · e · mo · ni · al (ser′ə mō′nē əl) *adj.* used in connection with a ceremony or some particular occasion.

chat · ter (chat′ər) *v.* to talk rapidly and foolishly, usually about matters of little importance.

chirp (churp) *v.* to make a short, sharp sound, such as that of a bird.

choc · o · late (chô′kə lit, chok′ə lit) *n.* a food made from ground and roasted cacao beans.

clue (kloo) *n.* a guide or key that aids in finding the solution to a problem or mystery.

---

a bad, ā cake, ä father; e pet, ē me; i it, ī ice; o hot, ō open, ô off; oo wood, oo food; oi oil, ou out; th thin, th that; u cup, ur turn, yoo music; zh treasure; ə ago, taken, pencil, lemon, helpful

coal (kōl) *n.*   a black or dark brown substance that burns easily and is widely used as a fuel.

cock · er span · iel (kok′ər span′yəl) a small dog with a flat or slightly waved dense coat of any of several colors.

code (kōd) *n.*   a system of writing used to keep messages secret, in which letters, symbols, or numbers stand for the letters and words of the message.

com · mon (com′ən) *adj.*   ordinary; average.

com · plaint (kəm plānt′) *n.*   an expression of dissatisfaction.

cop · per (kop′ər) *n.*   a reddish-brown metal that is easy to form in different shapes and is an excellent conductor of heat and electricity.

cork (kôrk) *n.*   **1.** the thick outer bark of a kind of oak tree. **2.** a stopper for a bottle made of cork.

cos · tume (kos′tōōm, kos′tyōōm) *n.*   clothing belonging to another time or place, worn on the stage, at parties, and so on.

cou · sin (kuz′in) *n.*   a son or daughter of one's uncle or aunt.

crease (krēs) *v.* **creased, creas · ing.**   to make or get a line or mark in by folding or wrinkling. —*n.*   a line or mark made by folding or wrinkling something.

crick · et (krik′it) *n.*   a hopping insect related to the grasshopper, having strong hind legs and long slender antennae.

croak (krōk) *v.*   to make a deep, hoarse sound.

Cub · ism (kyōō′biz′əm) *n.*   a movement in art, especially painting, begun in the early twentieth century, characterized by the use of basic geometric forms to represent objects.

curb (kurb) *n.*   a border of concrete, stone, or other material along the edge of a street or sidewalk; outer edge of a sidewalk.

cu · ri · ous (kyoor′ē əs) *adj.* eager to know or learn.

cus · to · di · an (kus tō′dē ən) *n.*   a person responsible for the care of a building; janitor.

364

D

dank (dangk) *adj.* disagreeably damp; moist and cold.

De·cem·ber (di sem′bər) *n.* the twelfth and last month of the year.

deck (dek) *v.* to dress or adorn; ornament.

de·light (di līt′) *v.* to give great pleasure or joy to; please highly.

de·mon (dē′mən) *n.* an evil spirit; devil.—*adj.* having the qualities of an evil spirit or devil.

de·sert·ed (di zur′tid) *adj.* abandoned.

de·serve (di zurv′) *v.* **de·served, de·serv·ing.** to have a right to; to be worthy of; merit.

de·tec·tive (di tek′tiv) *n.* a person who makes investigations to get evidence and information, especially in order to solve crimes and arrest criminals.

de·ter·mined (di tur′mind) *adj.* a person showing or having a fixed purpose; having one's mind made up.

dif·fi·cult (dif′ə kult′) *adj.* hard to do or perform; demanding effort; not easy.

di·rec·tions (di rek′shəns, dī rek′ shəns) *n. pl.* an order or instructions about how to proceed or act.

dis·ap·point (dis′ə point′) *v.* to fail to fulfill the hope, desire, or expectation of.

dis·cov·er·y (dis kuv′ə rē) *n. pl.,* **dis·cov·er·ies.** something that is seen or found for the first time.

dis·tance (dis′təns) *n.* the amount of space between two things, objects, or points.

dith·er (dith′ər) *n.* the condition of being stirred up, excited, or confused.

door·mat (dôr′mat′) *n.* a small, flat piece of material placed in front of a door, used by people coming in for wiping their feet.

dough (dō) *n.* a thick mixture of flour or meal, liquid, and other ingredients that is used to make bread, cookies, and other foods.

du·et (dōō et′, dyōō et′) *n.* a musical composition for two voices or instruments.

E

ea·gle (ē′gəl) *n.* any of a group of birds of prey related to the hawk.

a bad, ā cake, ä father; e pet, ē me; i it, ī ice; o hot, ō open, ô off; oo wood, ōō food; oi oil, ou out; th thin, <u>th</u> that; u cup, ur turn, yōō music; zh treasure; ə ago, taken, pencil, lemon, helpful

ear·phone (ēr′fōn′) *n.* a receiver held at or worn over the ear to listen.

ech·o (ek′ō) *v.* to be heard again.

em·bar·rass (em bar′əs) *v.* to cause to feel uncomfortable or ashamed.

en·cy·clo·pe·di·a (en sī′klə pē′dē ə) *n.* a book or set of books giving a great deal of information about many things.

en·e·my (en′ə mē) *n. pl.,* **en·e·mies.** a person or animal that dislikes or wishes to harm another.

e·nor·mous (i nôr′məs) *adj.* extremely large.

ex·act·ly (eg zakt′lē) *adv.* in the exact way; quite.

ex·claim (eks klām′) *v.* to speak or cry out suddenly, as in anger or surprise.

ex·tra (eks′trə) *adj.* more than what is usual, expected, or needed; additional.

F

fa·mil·iar (fə mil′yər) *adj.* often heard or seen.

fa·mous (fā′məs) *adj.* having great fame; well-known; renowned.

FBI Federal Bureau of Investigation, an agency of the United States Department of Justice that investigates violations of federal law.

fea·ture (fē′chər) *n.* a story, article, or column of special interest, appearing in a magazine or newspaper.

fer·ment (fər ment′) *v.* to go through a chemical change; to rot.

fid·dle (fid′əl) *n.* a violin or other instrument of the violin family.

fig (fig) *n.* a small, sweet fruit having many tiny seeds. Figs grow in the Mediterranean region and in California.

flash·bulb (flash′bulb′) *n.* a light used for taking photographs.

flesh (flesh) *n.* the soft part of the body of a human being or animal that covers the bones, consisting mainly of muscle and fat.

fol·ly (fol′ē) *n.* a lack of good sense; foolishness.

for·bid·den (fər bid′ən) *adj.* not permitted; prohibited.

for·tune (fôr′chən) *n.* something that happens or is going to happen to a person, whether good or bad; fate; luck.

fos·sil (fos′əl) *n.* the remains or traces of an animal or plant that lived long ago.

four·teen (fôr′tēn′) *n.* four more than ten.—*adj.* amounting to 14 in number.

glance (glans) *v.* **glanced, glanc·ing. 1.** to take a quick look. **2.** to hit something and move off at a slant.

grave (grāv) *n.* a hole dug in the earth for the burial of a body.

grav·el (grav′əl) *n.* pebbles and small pieces of rock.

guard (gärd) *n.* a person or group of persons that watches over or protects.

guest (gest) *n.* a person who is received by another, as for a party, meal, or visit.

G

gang (gang) *n.* a group of people who do things together.

gent·ly (jent′lē) *adv.* in a mild or kind way.

gla·cier (glā′shər) *n.* a large mass of ice moving slowly over land or down a valley.

H

hal·i·but (hal′ə bət) *n.* a large flatfish found in the Atlantic and Pacific oceans.

hand·some (han′səm) *adj.* having a pleasing, dignified appearance.

Har·le·quin (här′lə kwin, här′lə kin)

harm (härm) *n.* injury; hurt.

har·vest (här′vist) *n.* the gathering in of a crop when it is ripe.

---

a bad, ā cake, ä father; e pet, ē me; i it, ī ice; o hot, ō open, ô off; oo wood, o͞o food; oi oil, ou out; th thin, th that; u cup, ur turn, y o͞o music; zh treasure; ə ago, taken, pencil, lemon, helpful

hear (hēr) *v.* **heard, hear·ing.** to receive or be able to receive sound by means of the ear.

hel·i·cop·ter (hel′ ə kop′tər) *n.* an aircraft supported in the air by blades that rotate.

her·ring (her′ing) *n.* a bony, salt-water fish highly valued for food.

hiss (his) *v.* to make a sound like a prolonged *s*.

his·to·ry (his′tər ē) *n.* *pl.*, **his·to·ries.** the story or record of what has happened in the past.

hoard (hôrd) *n.* a supply that is stored or hidden away.

hoo·ray (hoo rā′) *interj.* a word used as an exclamation of joy, encouragement, or the like.

hor·rid (hôr′id, hor′id) *adj.* dreadful, shocking, or extremely unpleasant.

ho·tel (hō tǝl′) *n.* a place where travelers can rent rooms.

hy·drant (hī′drǝnt) *n.* a street fixture for drawing water directly from a water main, consisting of an upright pipe with spouts to which hoses can be attached.

I

ich·thy·o·saur (ik′thē ə sôr′) *n.* any of an extinct group of marine reptiles that resembled fish.

in·stinct (in′stingkt) *n.* a way of acting or behaving that a person or animal is born knowing.

in·tel·li·gent (in tel′ə jənt) *adj.* having or showing intelligence; bright; smart.

in·ter·est·ed (in′tris tid, in′tǝ res′tid) *adj.* having or showing concern or curiosity.

in·ven·tor (in ven′tər) *n.* a person who makes or invents a new device or process.

i·ron (ī ′ərn) *n.* a gray-white metal that is used in making steel.

J

jam (jam) *v.* **jammed, jam·ming.** to squeeze, force, or press into or through a tight or close space.—*n.* a mass of people or things crowded together.

K

ki·mo·no (ki mō′nə) *n.* a loose robe or gown that is tied with a sash.

L

la·dy (lā′dē) *n. pl.,* **la·dies. 1.** any woman. **2.** a woman of high social position. **3.** a girl or woman who is polite or has good manners.

latch (lach) *n.* any device for keeping a door, window, or gate closed.

loose (lo͞os) *adj.* not confined; free.

low·er·case (lō′ər kās′) *adj.* (of an alphabetic letter) of a form different from and smaller than its corresponding capital letter, as a, b, q, r.

M

mad·ame (mad′əm, mə dam′) *n.* a title of respect or form of polite address for a woman.

mad·e·moi·selle (mad′ə mə zel′) *n.* miss: a French form of address for an unmarried girl or woman.

mal·lard (mal′ərd) *n.* a common wild duck.

mi·cro·phone (mī′krə fōn′) *n.* a device that is used to transmit sound or make it louder.

min·now (min′ō) *n.* any of a group of freshwater fish widely used as bait.

mis·er·a·ble (miz′ər ə bəl) *adj.* very unhappy; wretched.

mis·er·a·bly (miz′ər ə blē) *adv.* very unhappily; wretchedly.

mist (mist) *n.* a mass or cloud of tiny droplets of water suspended in the air.

mis·take (mis tāk′) *n.* something incorrectly done, thought, or said.

molt (mōlt) *v.* to shed the hair, feathers, skin, or shell and replace with a new growth.

---

a bad, ā cake, ä father; e pet, ē me; i it, ī ice; o hot, ō open, ô off; oo wood, o͞o food; oi oil, ou out; th thin, th that; u cup, ur turn, yo͞o music; zh treasure; ə ago, taken, pencil, lemon, helpful

mo · ment (mō′mənt) *n.* a short period of time.

mus · cle (mus′əl) *n.* a body tissue made up of fibers that are used to make the body move.

mus · krat (musk′rat′) *n.* a small animal with dark brown fur. Muskrats live in and near the water.

N

na · tive (nā′tiv) *adj.* of, relating to, or characteristic of the original inhabitants of a region or country.

ninth (nīnth) *adj.* next after eighth.

numb (num) *adj.* lacking or having lost feeling or movement.

O

ob · sta · cle (ob′stə kəl) *n.* a person or thing that stands in the way, opposes, or blocks.

op · po · site (op′ə zit) *adj.* on the other side of or across from another person or thing; facing.

or · gan · i · za · tion (ôr′gə ni zā′shən) *n.* a group of people joined together for a particular purpose.

o · ri · ga · mi (ôr′i gä′mē) *n.* the Japanese art of folding paper into the forms of animals, flowers, or other objects.

P

pale (pāl) *adj.* having little light; not bright; dim.

par · rot (par′ət) *n.* a tropical bird having a hooked bill, large head, and glossy, colored feathers.

per · form (pər fôrm′) *v.* to carry out; do.

pe · ri · od (pir′ē əd) *n.* a portion of time of a given length or marked by certain events or conditions.

pho · to · graph (fō′tə graf′) *v.* to take a picture of.

Pi · cas · so, Pa · blo (pi kä′sō, pä′blō)

pi · geon (pij′ən) *n.* any of several wild or domesticated birds with a stout body, small head, and thick, soft feathers.

pig·sty (pig′stī′) *n.*   a place where pigs are kept; pigpen.

pi·ña·ta (pēn yä′tə) *n.*   a colorfully decorated container. It is filled with fruit and candy and hung from the ceiling to be broken with a stick by a blindfolded child.

po·lite (pə līt′) *adj.*   having good manners; showing a consideration for others; courteous.

pop·u·lar (pop′ yə lər) *adj.*   pleasing to or favored by very many or most people.

pour (pôr) *v.*   to flow in a steady stream.

pow·er (pou′ ər) *n.*   the ability or right to command, control, or make decisions; authority.

pre·pare (pri per′) *v.*   **pre·pared, pre·par·ing.**   to make or get ready.

prob·a·bly (prob′ ə blē) *adv.*   most likely; in all likelihood.

pro·nounce (prə nouns′) *v.*   to make the sound of a letter or word.

prop·er (prop′ər) *adj.*   correct or suitable for a certain purpose or occasion.

prove (prōov) *v.*   **proved, proved** or **prov·en, prov·ing.**   to show the truth or genuineness of.

pry (prī) *v.*   **pried, pry·ing.**   to move, raise, or pull by force; to get with much effort.

pu·pil (pyōo′pəl) *n.*   a person who studies under the direction of an instructor; student.

pure (pyoor) *adj.*   not mixed with anything else; not contaminated; clean.

pur·pose (pur′pəs) *n.*   the reason for which something is made or done. **on purpose.**   not by accident; deliberately.

Q

ques·tion (kwes′chən) *n.*   something asked in order to receive a reply or find out something.

R

ra·di·o (rā′dē ō′) *n.*   device for receiving radio broadcasts or for sending and receiving messages.

re·al·ize (rē′ə līz′) *v.*   **re·al·ized, re·al·iz·ing.**   to understand completely.

---

a bad, ā cake, ä father; e pet, ē me; i it, ī ice; o hot, ō open, ô off; oo wood,
ōo food; oi oil, ou out; th thin, th that; u cup, ur turn, yōo music; zh treasure;
ə ago, taken, pencil, lemon, helpful

re·cess (rē′ses, ri ses′) *n.* a period of time in which work or other activity is stopped temporarily.

re·flect (ri flekt′) *v.* **1.** to give back an image of. **2.** to serve to give a particular impression.

rep·tile (rep′til, rep′tīl′) *n.* any of a group of cold-blooded animals with backbones, including lizards, snakes, crocodiles, and turtles.

re·spon·si·bil·i·ty (ri spon′sə bil′ə tē) *n.* a job, duty, or area of concern.

re·tire (ri tīr′) *v.* **re·tired, re·tir·ing.** to withdraw oneself from public life, business, or active service.

ri·fle (rī′fəl) *n.* a firearm that is meant to be fired from the shoulder.

rock·ing chair (rok′ing chār) a chair that is mounted on rockers so that it can rock back and forth.

rule (rool) *n.* a direction or principle that serves as a guide for behavior or action.

S

sad·ness (sad′nis) *n.* unhappiness, sorrow, or gloom.

Sa·gan (sə gän′)

salm·on (sam′ən) *n.* a large fish with a silvery body used for food. Most salmon live in salt water but swim to fresh water to lay their eggs.

sat·is·fied (sat′is fīd′) *adj.* contented.

score (skôr) *n.* a record of points made in a game or contest.

screen (skrēn) *n.* anything that serves to separate, conceal, or protect.

search (surch) *n.* the act of looking or exploring carefully in order to find something.

sea·son (sē′zən) *n.* one of the divisions of the year (spring, summer, fall, winter), marked by differences in weather, temperature, and hours of daylight.

sec·re·tar·y (sek′rə ter′ē) *n.* a person employed to write letters, keep records, and the like for an individual or company.

sev·en-thir·ty (sev′ən thur′tē) *n.* half past seven; 7:30.

sew (sō) *v.* **sewed, sewed** or **sewn, sew·ing.** to make or mend by means of a needle and thread or sewing machine; to fasten or join with stitches.

shal·lows (shal'ōs) *n. pl.* an area in a body of water that is not deep.

shel·ter (shel'tər) *n.* something that covers or protects, as from weather, danger, or attack.

shiv·er (shiv'ər) *v.* to shake, as with cold or fear; tremble.

shy (shī) *adj.* uncomfortable in the presence of others; bashful; timid.

skel·e·ton (skel'ə tən) *n.* the framework of bones supporting the body of animal with a backbone.

skunk (skungk) *n.* an animal with black and white fur and a bushy tail. It sprays a bad-smelling liquid.

slate (slāt) *n.* a fine-grained, bluish-gray rock that splits easily into thin sheets or layers.

sly (slī) *adj.* secret; clever.

snow·capped (snō'kapt') *adj.* topped with snow.

soc·cer (sok'ər) *n.* a game in which the players try to move a round ball into a goal by kicking it with any part of their bodies except the hands and arms.

so·ci·e·ty (sə sī'ə tē) *n.* a group of people gathered together or associated for a common purpose or interest.

so·fa (sō'fə) *n.* a long, upholstered seat with a back and arms; couch.

sore (sôr) *n.* an area of the body where the skin is broken or bruised and painful or sensitive to the touch.

spi·der (spī'dər) *n.* a small animal with four pairs of legs, a body that is divided into two parts, and no wings.

spir·it (spir'it) *n.* a characteristic quality, mood, or tendency.

splen·did (splen'did) *adj.* impressive, brilliant, or glorious.

sprin·kler (spring'klər) *n.* a device that is used to water gardens and lawns.

a bad, ā cake, ä father; e pet, ē me; i it, ī ice; o hot, ō open, ô off; oo wood, o̅o̅ food; oi oil, ou out; th thin, th that; u cup, ur turn, yo̅o̅ music; zh treasure; ə ago, taken, pencil, lemon, helpful

squir · rel (skwur′əl) *n.* an animal related to the mouse, usually having a slender body and a long, bushy tail.

sta · tion (stā′shən) *n.* a building or place set up as the headquarters for a business or public service.

stead · y (sted′ē) *adj.* not changing; regular or uniform.

stiff · ly (stif′lē) *adv.* rigidly; with difficulty, as from cold, age, injury, or tiredness.

stink · bug (stingk′bug′) *n.* any of several insects that smell disagreeable.

strut (strut) *v.* **strut · ted, strut · ting.** to walk in a vain, pompous, or proud way.

stu · dent (stood′ənt, styood′ənt) *n.* a person who is going to school or who studies something.

stu · di · o (stoo′dē ō′, styoo′dē ō′) *n.* a place where an artist or a photographer works.

sug · ar (shoog′ ər) *n.* a white or brown sweet substance, usually in the form of small crystals or powder.

sug · gest (səg jest′) *v.* to offer or mention for consideration or action; propose.

sur · round (sə round′) *v.* to be on all sides of; form a circle around.

T

tax · i (tak′sē) *n.* an automobile that can be hired to take a person somewhere; taxicab.

tease (tēz) *v.* **teased, teas · ing.** to make fun of playfully or mischievously.

the · a · ter (thē′ə tər) *n.* a building or other place where plays, motion pictures, or other entertainments are presented.

there · fore (ther′fôr′) *adv.* consequently; as a result.

thump (thump) *n.* a beat or hit that makes a heavy, hollow sound.

toad (tōd) *n.* an animal that is like a frog.

trans · late (trans lāt′, trans′lāt′) *v.* **trans · lated, trans · lat · ing.** to change from one language into another.

tru · ly (troo′lē) *adv.* in a real, genuine, or honest way; sincerely.

tun·nel (tun′əl) *n.* a long, narrow, tubelike passageway beneath the ground or water.

tweed (twēd) *n.* a rough fabric usually made from wool, woven with yarns of two or more colors.

twelve (twelv) *n.* two more than ten; 12.—*adj.* amounting to 12 in number.

U

ul·ti·mate (ul′tə mit) *adj.* coming at the end; final.

up·ward (up′wərd) *adv.* from a lower to a higher place or position.

use·less (yo͞os′lis) *adj.* serving no use; having no purpose.

u·su·al·ly (yo͞o′zho͞o ə lē) *adv.* ordinarily; habitually.

V

vi·ta·min (vī′tə min) *n.* one of a group of substances needed in small amounts for the health and normal working of the body.

W

wad·dle (wod′əl) *v.* **wad·dled, wad·dling.** to walk or move with short steps, swaying from side to side.

wal·rus (wôl′rəs, wol′rəs) *n.* a large animal that lives in water in the Arctic. The walrus looks like a seal but is larger.

waste (wāst) *v.* **wast·ed, wast·ing.** to use or spend in a careless or useless way.

Wednes·day (wenz′dē, wenz′dā) *n.* the fourth day of the week.

whack (hwak) *n.* a sharp, resounding blow.

whose (ho͞oz) *pron.* the possessive case of *who* and *which*.

wink (wingk) *v.* to close and open one eyelid very quickly.

wool·ly (wool′ē) *adj.* covered with soft, thick, curly hair or something of a similar texture.

Y

yes·ter·day (yes′tər dē, yes′tər dā′) *n.* the day before today.

---

a bad, ā cake, ä father; e pet, ē me; i it, ī ice; o hot, ō open, ô off; oo wood, o͞o food; oi oil, ou out; th thin, th that; u cup, ur turn, yo͞o music; zh treasure; ə ago, taken, pencil, lemon, helpful